Emergency Care for Cats and Dogs

FIRST AID FOR YOUR PET

Craton Burkholder,
D.V.M., M.A.

MICHAEL KESEND PUBLISHING, LTD.
New York

To good pets who compliment our lives.

The ideas, procedures and suggestions contained in this book are not intended as a substitute for consulting with your veterinarian.

Cover design: Kim Llewellyn
Illustrations: Sue Eldenberg and Sarah A. Pletts

First Printing: 1987, Fourth Printing: 1991

Burkholder, Craton R.
Emergency care for cats and dogs.
Bibliography: p.

1. Dogs—Diseases. 2. Cats—Diseases. 3. Veterinary emergencies. 4. First aid for animals. I. Title.
SF991.B87 1987 636.7'0896025 87-3726

ISBN 0-935576-18-5 (paper)
ISBN 0-935576-19-3 (hardcover)

CONTENTS

ACKNOWLEDGEMENTS

I am particularly grateful to my good friend Dr. Donald F. McCann, not only for the time he spent reviewing the book, but also for his encouragement and recommendations. I am greatly indebted to the contributions of my reviewers, Dr. Stephen I. Bistner, Dr. Robert L. Maahs, Dr. Richard A. Deitrich, Dr. John A. Mulnix, Dr. Wayne E. Wingfield. I am especially appreciative to my wife, Mardell, for her helpful suggestions and the preparation of the manuscript.

The contributions of my staff deserve special note since without them this book would not have been possible.

FOR ALL EMERGENCIES
SEE CENTER INDEX PAGES 94 AND 95

INTRODUCTION

In a serious emergency first aid cannot take the place of a veterinarian's professional services. Knowing how to provide proper assistance in an emergency, however, will influence the outcome of the case and will, in many instances, save an animal's life.

There is a time to assist your animals yourself, a time to telephone your veterinarian and a time to seek professional assistance immediately. The purpose of this book is to help you select the proper action and hopefully, to give you assistance in those infrequent situations when you are unable to get your pet to a veterinarian. There will be occasions when no first aid treatment is appropriate and only veterinary services can be helpful. It is hoped that this book will enable you to better distinguish between the two.

EMERGENCY INFORMATION

VETERINARIAN

Name:
Address:

Telephone-office:
Telephone-home:

HOSPITAL

Name:
Address:

Telephone:

OTHER EMERGENCY TELEPHONE NUMBERS

Veterinary Society (emergency):

Local Humane Society:

Public Health Officer:

Animal Shelter:

Poison Control Center:*

Sheriff/Police:

*This telephone number is available from your local human hospital.

PET'S LICENSE NUMBER

Name:	Number:
Name:	Number:
Name:	Number:

IMMUNIZATION RECORD

Date	Pet's Name	Vaccination

MEDICAL HISTORY

Date	Pet's Name

MEDICAL RECORD

Date

NORMAL VALUES

	Rectal Temperature	Heart Rate	Respiratory Rate
Cats	$101.5 \pm 1°F$	160 - 240 per minute	20-30 per minute
Dogs	$101.5 \pm 1°F$	70 - 160 per minute	10-30 per minute

Suggested First Aid Kit and Uses

Item	General Use Examples
Adhesive tape, 1 in. (1)	Use in bandaging and restraint
Antibiotic ointment or powder	Treating wounds
Antibiotic opthalmic ointment	Protecting injured and infected eyes
Antiseptic (Povidone iodine solution, etc.)	Disinfectant for wounds, instruments
Cotton, absorbent	Cleaning wounds when moistened, cleaning eyes and ears, removing external parasites, etc.
Cotton swab sticks	Cleaning wounds, eyes, ears, etc.
Gauze dressing pads	
sterile (8)	Protecting wounds
nonsterile (16)	Cleaning wounds with disinfectant
Gauze rolls, 1 and 2 in. (1 each)	Secure wound dressings, muzzle injured dogs, making gauze pads when folded
Ipecac syrup (1 container)	Induce vomiting in cases of suspected poisoning
Scissors, blunt pointed	Use in bandaging, cutting hair
Thermometer, rectal	Taking temperatures
Tweezers	Removing splinters, dirt from wounds or ticks
Vaseline or petroleum jelly	Thermometer lubrication

Household Items Useful For First Aid

Item	General Use Examples
Blankets	Keeping animals warm, transporting injured animals
Diapers (disposable or regular)	Use as a compress to control bleeding, bandages or padding for splints
Empty plastic gallon containers	Holding hot water for shock treatment
Eye dropper	Fluid administration
Flashlight	Treatment in the dark
Magazines, newspapers, pillows	Use as emergency splints, place under animal on cold or wet ground
Paper cups	Giving fluids, washing wounds
Pliers	Removing porcupine quills and fishhooks
Safety pins	Securing bandages
Sanitary napkins	Use as a compress to control bleeding, bandages or padding for splints
Soap, mild white	Cleaning wounds, scratches, etc.
Table leaf	Stretcher for head, neck and back injuries
Tape (electrical, masking, etc.)	Use in bandaging and restraint
Towels or sheets	Use as a compress to control bleeding, bandages or padding for splints
Wooden paint mixing sticks	Use as emergency splint

Household Medications Useful for First Aid

Items	General Use Examples
Antibacterial ointments (Neosporin, Betadine)	Use for skin infections or wounds
Aspirin or aspirin substitutes	Use for fever or pain relief (see text)
Calamine lotion	Soothe skin irritation
Hydrogen peroxide (3%)	Induce vomiting (see text)
Kaolin-pectin solution (Kaopectate)	Use for diarrhea and some poisonings
Milk of Magnesia	Use as an antacid, laxative for constipation, and some poisonings (see text)
Pepto-Bismol	Use to coat stomach and aid in the control of vomiting and diarrhea (see text)
Vitamin A and D ointment	Use to help heal superficial wounds and soothe irritated skin

#1 Abdominal Distension

There are several reasons for an acutely distended abdomen and the degree of importance varies with its severity and cause. Simple overeating is common in puppies and kittens and is normally not serious. However, gastric dilatation and volvulus (twisting) is the utmost emergency! Abdominal distentions which need emergency treatment include severe overeating, overdrinking, air swallowing and gastric dilatation and volvulus.

OVEREATING OR OVERDRINKING

All breeds of any age are susceptible to overeating and overdrinking but it occurs more commonly in kittens and puppies or in animals that have not eaten regular meals.

Causes

- Consumption of large quantities of food (deer or elk carcasses during hunting season)
- Eating garbage
- Excessive water consumption following ingestion of large quantities of dry dog food
- Excessive water consumption following exercise or the unavailability of water for abnormally long periods of time

Signs

- Swollen abdomen
- Possible vomiting or retching
- Groaning

Treatment

- Refer to treatment under Gastric Dilatation and Volvulus

AIR SWALLOWING (Aerophagia)

Causes

- Excitement, nervousness, gulping food or water, exercise, or sore throat can elicit the abnormal swallowing of air

Signs

- Swollen abdomen
- Gulping of air or continuous swallowing
- Retching and/or belching

Treatment

- The few cases that show discomfort may require treatment. The underlying causes should be determined by a veterinarian and eliminated

GASTRIC DILATATION AND VOLVULUS

Synonyms

Canine bloat, gastric torsion, gastric dilatation/volvulus (GDV)

Definition

Gastric dilatation and volvulus is seen most often in large breeds and deep chested dogs.

Commonly affected dogs are Great Danes, Irish Wolfhounds, Saint Bernards, Great Pyrenees, Poodles, Newfoundlands, Weimaraners, Bloodhounds, Boxers and Irish Setters. The accumulation of gas in the stomach causes distention and a concurrent twisting of the stomach on its axis (volvulus). Its exact cause is unknown, but there is interference with blood circulation and shock, coma and death can occur within 2 or 3 hours. It is believed that the distention occurs before the twisting and may or may not follow ingestion of a large meal.

Signs

- Enlarged abdomen
- Abdomen is painful, especially when touched, and may sound tympanic if thumped with the forefinger
- Excess salivation with unsuccessful attempts at vomiting
- Difficult breathing
- Evidence of shock (See Section #26 — Shock)
- Reluctance to move and often refusal to lie down until collapsing
- Once they lie down they usually will not move

Treatment

IMPORTANT — Animals with severe abdominal distension and respiratory distress must receive immediate veterinary attention.

- Prevent further access to food or water

- Keep quiet and provide plenty of fresh air
- Do not attempt further treatment — Seek veterinary assistance immediately

Prevention

NOTE — Overeating and gastric dilatation/volvulus both have a tendency to reoccur and preventative measures should be taken.

Overeating or Drinking

- Do not allow puppies or kittens free access to all the food or liquid, i.e., milk, they desire (See Section #15 — Diarrhea)
- Prevent access to such things as garbage and animal carcasses
- Avoid excessive water consumption following exercise or the unavailability of water.

Gastric Dilatation and Volvulus

- Give several small daily feedings (3 to 4 times per day)
- Feed moistened food and allow free access to water
- Avoid strenuous exercise or excitement immediately before or after eating or drinking
- Avoid access to such things as garbage and animal carcasses

#2 Bleeding

MANAGEMENT OF EXTERNAL BLEEDING

- Use proper restraint and avoid excitement (See Section #35 — Restraint/Transportation)
- First try to control bleeding by direct pressure or a pressure bandage (see ilustration on next page and explanation)
- Apply a tourniquet as a last report — only if blood loss becomes critical (see illustration and explanation)
- Seek veterinary assistance for serious bleeding, further examination and treatment

Severe bleeding must receive immediate attention regardless of what other injuries are present. Bleeding from minor cuts and wounds generally stops within a few minutes. Profuse external bleeding resulting from blood vessel damage can usually be controlled by applying firm, direct pressure over the wound with a sterile or clean gauze or cloth such as a handkerchief or t-shirt (see illustration).

Arterial blood will flow irregularly in time with the heartbeat and will be bright red; whereas, blood from a vein will flow evenly and be dark red. Apply additional pressure between the heart and the wound for bleeding from an artery and below the wound for a vein.

Application of a pressure bandage is normally the safest and best way to stop bleeding. Apply a

APPLICATION OF DIRECT
PRESSURE TO A WOUND

sterile or clean gauze, cloth, or sanitary napkin directly over the wound and bandage the area firmly with a 2 or 3 inch gauze roll. Torn strips of cloth approximately 3 inches across by 4 feet long made from a bedding sheet or soft material can serve very well. Secure the gauze in place with adhesive, electrical or masking tape, or by tying the gauze or cloth. Avoid frequent removal of the bandage to check the wound because bleeding may start again.

Application of a tourniquet should be reserved for bleeding that cannot be controlled by direct pressure, such as a severely mangled or crushed leg or tail. A tourniquet made of 2-inch-wide gauze bandage, cloth or necktie should be applied directly above the wound and should be released every 10 minutes. When properly adjusted there should be oozing from the wound and you should be able to place a finger under the bandage when it is in place (See Section #16—Bandaging/Splints/Collars). Do not apply a tourniquet unless it is absolutely necessary.

IMPORTANT — Bleeding from the ear, foot pad or penis can result in fatal hemorrhaging and the potential seriousness of these types of cuts cannot be overemphasized. Normal clotting of blood in an ear injury is prevented by the whip-like action of the ear during head shaking. Prevent this by binding the head with a roll of gauze and tape or use a nylon or knee sock with the bottom cut out (See illustration page 85). A bleeding foot pad should have a pressure bandage applied.

Hemorrhaging from the penis can frequently be slowed or controlled by applying cold compresses to the area. A female in season will excite the

PROPER TOURNIQUET APPLICATION

male causing an erection which can result in uncontrollable hemorrhaging. Remove the male from the area to avoid this complication.

MANAGEMENT OF INTERNAL BLEEDING

- Seek veterinary assistance
- Treat for shock (See Section #26 — Shock)
- Do not give the animal anything to eat or drink

IMPORTANT — Internal hemorrhage should be considered a possibility following any sharp blow or injury to the abdomen or chest. This is especially true if hit by an automobile.

Severe bleeding will cause the animal to show signs of shock and should be treated accordingly. Coughing up bright, red, foamy blood indicates injury to the mouth, trachea or lungs. Vomit or excrement that is a bright red to dark reddish-brown (coffee-color) may indicate injury to the stomach or intestines.

Notes

#3 Burns/Smoke Inhalation

3.

Burns are classified by the extent and depth of the injury. Superficial or minor burns are ones that do not extend below the skin. Deep or major burns extend through the skin and involve the underlying tissues. Most burns are caused by friction, direct heat, scalding and flames. Electrical and chemical burns are other types that are not uncommon.

SUPERFICIAL OR MINOR BURNS

Signs

- Singed hair
- Redness of the skin
- Mild swelling
- Blistering
- Touching causes pain

Treatment

Painful lesions may require anesthesia before treatment can be performed.

- Prevent licking and scratching of burns
- Apply cold water or cold compresses for 15 minutes
- Gently remove overlying hair
- Cleanse the area with a very mild soap and water or flush with clean distilled water
- Apply a topical antibiotic ointment
- Apply dressings or clean gauze pads and bandage. An elastic bandage is excellent if care is taken not to wrap too tightly

- Protective medication for use on foot pad abrasions can be obtained from your veterinarian. Recently torn foot pads usually require suturing and/or bandaging.

DEEP OR MAJOR BURNS

Signs

- Singed hair
- Redness of the skin
- Fluid loss from the skin and underlying tissues
- Charred tissues with areas insensitive to a pin prick
- Reluctance to move
- Resistance to handling

IMPORTANT — Do not contribute to further contamination of the burns. Cover the wounds with a clean cloth while transporting the animal.

Treatment

Moderate and severe burns should always receive veterinary treatment. Most major wounds become infected. Thorough cleaning should be delayed and undertaken only under aseptic conditions. These wounds are very painful and anesthesia is usually required.

- Keep quiet
- Prevent licking, scratching or rubbing of the burn wounds
- Bandage the involved area and apply a plastic bucket or collar if necessary to keep

the animal away from the wounds (See Section #16 — Bandaging/Splints/Collars)

- Use physical restraint if necessary (See Section #35 — Restraint/Transportation)
- Treat for shock if present (See Section #26 — Shock)
- Apply sterile, dry gauze and bandages where possible
- Seek veterinary assistance
- Administer a saline solution orally if professional treatment is to be delayed 12 hours or more. Mix 2 level teaspoons of table salt and 1 level teaspoon of baking soda in 3 pints of water. Give at a rate equal to l0% of the body weight of the dog the first day and 5% the second day. Example: A 60 pound dog would require 3 quarts of the solution over the first 24 hour period since 1 pint of water is approximately 1 pound.

NOTE — Do not apply ointments to severe burns

Complications

- Smoke inhalation is a potential complication regardless of the severity of the burn
- Infection
- Pneumonia
- Acute liver or kidney disease
- Scar formation

ELECTRICAL BURNS

Causes

- Chewing an electrical cord
- Lightning

Signs

- Reddish or charred wounds of the mouth, tongue and lips
- Dead, discolored tissue if the injury happened several days earlier
- Difficult breathing

Treatment

IMPORTANT — Turn the current off or cautiously unplug the electrical cord from the outlet.

- Gently clip and cleanse the area
- Apply a topical antibiotic ointment
- If breathing has stopped, administer artificial respiration (See Section #7 — Drowning/Artificial Respiration)
- Treat for shock if present (See Section #26 — Shock)

Complications

- Infection
- Interference with breathing and swallowing

CHEMICAL BURNS

Causes

Contact with corrosive chemicals usually

occurs around a storage area such as a garage, basement or closet and results from accidental spillage by someone or the pet itself. Examples of corrosive materials are battery acid and some toilet bowl cleaners.

Signs

- Redness of the skin or lips
- Painful areas
- Squinting and pawing of eyes (See Section #8 — Ear/Eye Injuries)

Treatment

- Flush the area immediately with large quantities of water
- Acids — Bathe the area in a diluted sodium bicarbonate solution (baking soda)
- Alkalis — Bathe the area in a solution made by mixing equal parts of vinegar and water or lemon juice and water
- Apply a topical antibiotic ointment and bandage

FRICTION BURNS

Automobile accidents cause injuries from being hurled or dragged along the pavement, resulting in friction burns and abrasion wounds. Foot pads can be worn down easily from abrasive wear when dogs follow their owner's car or bicycle on pavement. Playing ball or other activities on concrete or asphalt areas will likewise severely wear the pad surfaces down. Rope abrasions are also friction burns.

DIRECT HEAT

Severe foot pad and skin burns result from walking in freshly poured asphalt or tar (See Section #17 — Grooming). Similar burns result from cats walking over hot stove burner surfaces, licking barbeque grills or eating dry food to which very hot water has been added. This may cause serious burns of the tongue, mouth, esophagus and stomach. Many other forms of radiant heat burns are possible.

SCALD BURNS

Hot liquids such as water, broth and fat can cause scalding injuries. Pets seeking food near the kitchen stove are common victims.

FLAME BURNS

The most common example of flame burns results from pets trapped in burning buildings. Contact with flammable liquids which in turn catch fire following an automobile accident or a deliberate dousing and igniting by someone are regrettable but not unheard of.

SMOKE INHALATION

History

Recent entrapment in a smoke filled environment

Signs

- Coughing with or without producing blood
- Cyanosis or blue lips and tongue (See illustration page 127)
- Weakness or unconsciousness

Treatment

- Administer oxygen by face mask if available. Treat for shock (See Section #26 — Shock)
- Provide humidified air for breathing. Example: Use commercial vaporizers or steam from a hot shower in a bathroom
- Seek veterinary assistance

NOTE — Smoke inhalation victims may show no outward evidence of illness, but can develop fatal complications within a matter of two to three days.

Complications

- Pulmonary edema (fluid in the lungs)
- Pneumonia

References: 1, 3

Notes

#4 Cardiac Arrest
Cardiopulmonary Resuscitation

Cardiopulmonary resuscitation (CPR) consists of a combination of external cardiac massage and artificial respiration. This is an emergency procedure used when there is no pulse or heartbeat. Irreversible brain damage will occur within 3 to 4 minutes once cardiac arrest is present.

CARDIAC ARREST

Causes

- Severe injuries with shock
- Drowning
- Electrical Shock
- Heart diseases

Signs

- Unconsciousness
- No breathing movements
- No pulse
- No femoral artery pulse can be felt (See illustration Page 39)
- No heart beat can be felt with your hand or heard when your ear is placed on the chest wall (See illustration Page 39)
- No respiration is present

CARDIOPULMONARY RESUSCITATION (CPR)

IMPORTANT — External cardiac massage

should be accompanied by mouth-to-nose respiration. More effective CPR can be performed by two people.

- Lay the animal on its side on a firm surface
- Extend the head and neck, pull the tongue forward and remove any foreign material present — A piece of cloth is useful for holding the tongue and for wiping the air passage clean

Two Person Resuscitation (See illustrations Page 37)

- One person should start mouth to nose respiration (l5 times per minute or one time for each four to six chest compressions). Watch the chest expand each time to verify effectiveness
- The second person should place their hand or hands on the lower one half of the chest immediately behind the elbow. Apply cardiac massage by compressing the chest 1 to 2 inches at a minimum rate of 60 times per minute, i.e., compress for a count of 2 and release for a count of 1

IMPORTANT — Note pulse to determine effectiveness of chest compressions. There should be an approximate 1 to 4 ratio between respiration and cardiac massage. In very small animals (1 to 5 lbs.), one hand should be placed around the chest and cardiac massage applied.

One Person Resuscitation (See illustrations Page 38)

- Place your knee behind the animal's head, cup its mouth and nostrils with one hand and administer mouth-to-nose respiration through a cupped hand. It is not necessary for one's mouth to touch animal's nose. (15 times per minute)
- Using the other hand, apply cardiac massage by compressing the chest wall (60-80 times per minute)
- Use oxygen if available
- Seek veterinary assistance when the pulse and respiration return or continue resuscitation attempts while on your way to the hospital — have someone call ahead

TWO PERSON RESUSCITATION
CARDIAC MASSAGE

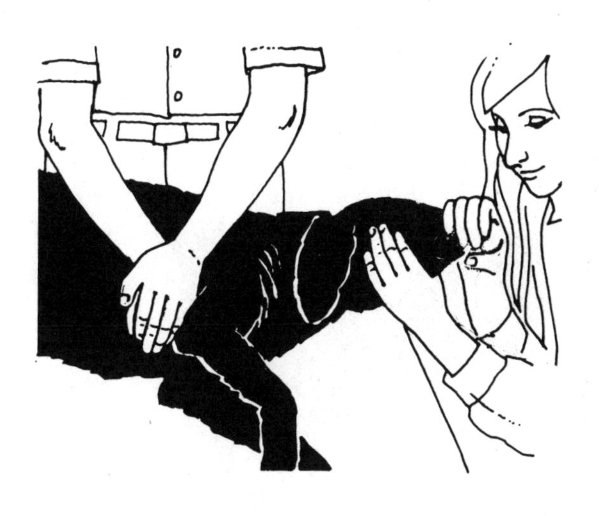

MOUTH-TO-NOSE RESPIRATION
CARDIAC MASSAGE

CHECKING FOR A HEART BEAT

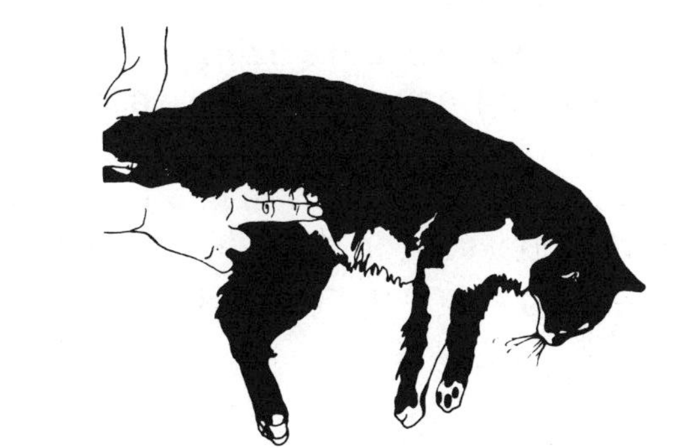

FEELING A FEMORAL ARTERY PULSE

#5 Choking

A true obstruction of the throat is rare in small animals, but dangerous when it does occur, it occurs most commonly in puppies or some Brachycephalic (short-headed) breeds such as Boxers, Boston Bull Terriers or Bulldogs. The presence of foreign bodies or wounds in the mouth or throat that do not obstruct the air passage are much more common.

5.

OBSTRUCTION OF THE THROAT

Causes

- Objects such as rubber balls and pieces of meat lodged in the back of the pharynx or esophagus
- Throat edema or swelling caused by insect stings or infection
- Allergic reactions in small breeds of dogs (l0 to 25 lbs.) causes throat swelling. These cases usually follow excitement or exercise and resolve themselves in a few minutes
- The ingestion or inhalation of something irritating is one of the most likely causes in cats

Signs

- Sudden difficult breathing
- Cyanosis or blue lips and tongue (See illustration page 127)
- Collapse

Treatment

- Pull the tongue forward and inspect the throat
- Hold the mouth open and carefully remove the object by grasping it firmly
- Strike the side of the rib cage firmly with the palm of your hand 3 to 4 times while the animal is laying on its side. Stand behind a large dog and lift up its forelegs while giving 3 or 4 forceful compressions on both sides of the chest
- Repeat if necessary
- Unconscious animals should have the tongue pulled well forward and maintained in that position. This is especially true in Brachycephalic breeds.
- Give artificial respiration if necessary
- Start mouth-to-nose respiration by cupping one hand over the nose while holding the lips and mouth closed. Remove your mouth between breaths and look and listen for air leaving the lungs. Repeat regularly at 5 second intervals. If the heartbeat stops or no pulse can be felt on the underside of the hindleg, start chest compression massage. Lay the animal on its side and push down forcefully on the rib cage with one hand 60-80 times per minute (See Section #4—Cardiac Arrest—Cardiopulmonary Resuscitation)

FOREIGN BODIES IN THE MOUTH OR ESOPHAGUS

Causes

- Objects such as bones and sticks frequently lodge in the roof of the mouth between the upper teeth

- Wounds, growths or infection of the tongue, throat or tonsils
- Fish hooks or needles may lodge at the base of the tongue or the roof of the mouth

Signs

- Apprehension
- Choking or gagging
- Salivation or spitting up white or blood-tinged phlegm
- Pawing at the mouth
- Rubbing the side of the head on the ground

Treatment

- Press the thumb and forefingers of one hand into the upper cheeks forcing the mouth to open wide. Gently remove the object with your fingers or a pair of long-nosed pliers
- If wounds exist or a foreign body cannot be removed easily and is embedded in the tissue, seek veterinary assistance

Prevention

- Restrict access to rubber toys that can be chewed up easily or are of a size that, if swallowed, can be wedged in the esophagus easily
- Feed meat chunks that are either very small or are in large pieces in order to prevent

swallowing whole

- Brachycephalic breeds of dogs that have a difficult time breathing should be checked by your veterinarian

#6 Convulsions

Convulsions or seizures are violent, involuntary contractions or a series of contractions of the voluntary muscles. They are either acquired (secondary to some other cause) or congenital (those suspected to be of an inherited nature). There are many causes of convulsions. The primary concern is not to determine its cause but to administer appropriate care for the animal. Minor seizures may last from a few seconds to a minute or two, with or without the loss of consciousness. Major seizures last from a few minutes to several minutes and are characterized by the apparent loss of consciousness.

Signs

- Restlessness with a frightened or dazed appearance
- Pets may either hide, seek affection or wander
- Head shaking with facial muscle twitching
- Salivation and foaming at the mouth
- Licking the lips and snapping the jaws
- Dilated pupils
- Loss of consciousness
- Violent muscle twitching and contractions sometimes with rapid leg movements
- Greatly increased respiratory rate
- Loss of urine and bowel control

NOTE — Immediately following a seizure there is a period of confusion, disorientation, pacing, salivation, unresponsiveness to external stimuli, weakness and temporary visual impairment.

Treatment

An animal with convulsions can be frightening and upsetting. Remain as calm as possible and intervene only as indicated. Treatment is limited to preventing injury to the animal and to yourself. During a convulsion an animal has no conscious control over its actions. A completely effective treatment for a convulsion at the time it happens is not practical since it involves an intravenous injection of an anticonvulsant medication.

IMPORTANT — Continuous seizures require immediate medical attention. Poisons are a common cause of convulsions and should be treated accordingly (See Section #24 — Poisons).

- Do not physically restrain
- Keep children away and stay back yourself
- Never place fingers between the teeth
- Do not attempt to give anything to drink during a seizure
- Make the animal comfortable
- Keep it on the floor and prevent it from falling down a staircase or off a bed or table
- Keep the area free of hard or sharp objects
- Use a blanket or coat for padding and protection
- Keep the area quiet with minimal lighting
- Administer artificial respiration if breathing stops by cupping one hand over the nose while holding the lips and mouth closed. Remove your mouth between breaths and look and listen for air leaving the lungs. Repeat regularly at 5 second intervals. If the heartbeat stops or no pulse can be felt on the underside of the hindleg, start chest

compression massage. Lay the animal on its side and push down forcefully on the rib cage with one hand 60 - 80 times per minute (See Section #4—Cardiac Arrest)

- Contact a veterinarian. Pets developing a convulsion for the first time, regardless of the cause, should be examined

Notes

#7 Drowning/Artificial Respiration

Causes

Most animals swim instinctively and can stay afloat for long periods of time. Some Bulldogs, very young puppies, kittens and injured animals may not be very effective swimmers. Drownings usually occur when animals become exhausted. Falling into a swimming pool or pond which has steep sides, or being caught in a strong current may prevent the animal from pulling itself out of the water.

Treatment

- Remove any foreign matter from the nose and mouth
- Drain the mouth and nose by holding the animal upside down by the hindlegs for a few seconds. This is especially effective in salt water drownings
- Start mouth-to-nose respiration (artificial respiration) by cupping one hand over the nose while holding the lips and mouth closed (see illustration Page 38). Remove your mouth between breaths and look and listen for air leaving the lungs. Repeat regularly at 5-second intervals. If the heartbeat stops or no pulse can be felt on the underside of the hindleg (see illustrations page 39), proceed to:

- Use chest compression massage. Lay the animal on its side and push down forcefully on the rib cage with one hand. Repeat at 5-second intervals (See Section #4—Cardiac Arrest). A second person can extend the neck and pull the tongue forward as well as supplement with oxygen, if available.

Reference: 22

#8 Ear/Eye Injuries

EAR INJURIES

Causes

Wounds such as bites and barbed wire

- Foreign bodies inside the ear canal such as grass awns and seeds which are often referred to as foxtails
- Insects inside the ear canal such as ticks, ear mites or small flying bugs — Ear mites are common in cats
- Infections (bacterial and fungal) are especially prevalent in dogs with long drooping ears and those with hair growing inside the ear canal

Signs

- Violent head shaking
- Scratching at the ears or neck
- Dragging an ear along the floor
- Tilting the affected side down
- Tenderness when handled around the head and neck
- Unusual odor
- Discharge from the ear canal
- Swelling of the ear

Treatment

IMPORTANT — A dog can lose large amounts of blood from a minor wound due to continual head shaking that prevents clotting.

Wounds

- Control bleeding by applying pressure directly to the wound with a clean gauze or cloth. The use of cold water will slow bleeding
- Apply a head bandage (see text page 85 and illustration Section 16— Bandaging/Splints/Collars) to maintain pressure and prevent head shaking
- Many wounds require suturing which will usually necessitate an anesthetic
- Whenever you cannot get to a veterinarian or if the wound is minor, clip the hair, clean with a mild antiseptic, and apply an antibiotic ointment

Foreign Bodies and Insects

- A grass awn or seed, when visible, may be removed gently
- Do not probe or remove anything from deep within the ear
- Living insects are sometimes attracted to light and can be induced to crawl out by holding a bright light close to the ear
- Temporary relief of pain can be provided by pouring a bland oil such as mineral, baby or olive oil directly into the ear canal. Visible material may be removed with an ear swab. **NOTE** — Foreign bodies and insects deep in the ear must be removed by a veterinarian

Infections

- Examination, diagnosis and treatment are required by a veterinarian

Deep injury to the ear

- Loosely place a small piece of cotton in the outer ear canal and seek veterinary assistance

Prevention

- Breeds of dogs such as poodles, terriers and spaniels that have hair within their ear canals should have it routinely pulled or cut out. Hair tends to retain moisture and increases the chances of infection
- Ears may be wiped out and flushed with rubbing alcohol periodically
- During a routine exam, have a veterinarian verify that your pet has normal ears. Alcohol should not be used when an acutely inflamed or perforated eardrum exists

Complications

- Animals, especially cats, may mutilate themselves, resulting in infection and abscesses
- Hematomas are accumulations of blood between the cartilage and skin of the ear and may develop secondary to excessive head shaking and scratching. Surgical treatment is usually required

EYE INJURIES

IMPORTANT — Proper initial emergency care not only relieves pain but may also prevent permanent loss of vision.

Causes

- Foreign bodies such as grass awns (foxtails), sawdust and pieces of straw and dirt are all potential sources
- Lacerations and contusions result from fights, automobile accidents, blows, kicks and cat scratches
- Chemical irritants such as acids or alkalis are likely causes of eye injury
- A prolapsed eyeball is more commonly seen in short-nosed breeds of dogs and usually results from fights or automobile accidents

Signs

Foreign bodies, Lacerations and Chemicals

- Rubbing and pawing of the eyes
- Eye tightly shut
- Eyelids swollen
- Watering of the eyes
- Spasms of the eyelids
- Eyes sensitive to light

Prolapsed Eyeball

- Eyeball hanging from the socket
- Hemorrhagic, inflamed and congested tissues

- The surface of the eye becomes dry
- Pain and discomfort are present

Treatment

Since the eyes are very delicate organs almost all injuries should be examined promptly by a veterinarian.

IMPORTANT — Animals with eye injuries must be restrained to prevent further injury.

Foreign Bodies

- Separate the eyelids and carefully examine the eye
- Remove obvious foreign bodies very gently with the tip of a moistened cotton swab, clean handkerchief or cloth.

IMPORTANT

— No attempt should be made to remove an object closely adherent to the surface of the eye

- Irrigate the eye with a household eyewash (or a 2% boric acid solution). Avoid touching or wiping the eyeball
- Seek veterinary attention

Lacerations and Contusions

- Lacerations of the eye may appear serious, but as long as the eyeball itself is not involved, vision will remain normal. Loss of vision can, however, occur from a laceration of the eyeball

Eyelids

- To control bleeding apply direct pressure to the lids. Cold compresses are helpful
- The eye can then be left alone or a protective gauze and head bandage may be applied without pressure until veterinary assistance is obtained

Eyeball

- Repeated use of cold compresses will tend to stop or prevent further bleeding
- Cover both eyes with a loose bandage. Movement of the uninjured eye will result in undesired movement of the injured eye
- Steady the animal's head by any means necessary to prevent further injury to the eye by the animal itself
- Do not apply pressure to a lacerated eyeball
- Do not remove a protruding foreign body from the eye

NOTE — Hemorrhage in the white portion of the eye (sclera) usually clears in a couple of weeks. However, it suggests the possibility of a more serious injury inside the eye which should be checked by a veterinarian.

Chemical Irritants

- Holding the lids open, flush the eye immediately with water for 10 to 15 minutes. Do not let the water run into the uninjured eye
- Seek veterinary assistance promptly

Prolapsed Eyeball

- Replacement of the eye must be performed quickly to prevent loss of vision and the eye itself
- Keep the eye moist with water, preferably distilled water
- Treat for shock (See Section #26 — Shock)
- Seek veterinary assistance immediately
- Do not force the eyeball back into the socket. If you cannot obtain veterinary services within an hour, attempt the following: Lubricate the eyeball with a few drops of olive or mineral oil and gently draw the lids outward over the eyeball. No force should be used.

Notes

#9 Electric Shock

Cause

- Biting through live wires such as electrical cords or blankets
- Direct contact with electrical wires
- Lightening

Signs

- Violent muscle contractions with the inability to release an electrically charged object
- Collapse and unconsciousness
- No evidence of a heart beat or pulse
- No breathing
- Cyanosis or blue lips and tongue (See illustration page 127)
- Signs of shock (See Section #26 — Shock)
- Burns

Treatment

The first step is to separate the animal from the electrical source. It is very important not to touch the animal directly or use an object that conducts electricity or is wet. Shut off the current at a circuit breaker or fuse box. Disconnect an electrical cord from its connection. Push away with a dry pole or board while standing on something dry (blanket, rubber mat, or newspaper). After separating proceed to:

- Re-establish the heart beat and breathing immediately

- Give cardiopulmonary resuscitation (See Section #4 — Cardiac Arrest)
- Treat for shock (See Section #26 — Shock)
- Treat for burns (See Section #3 — Burns/Smoke Inhalation)

Complications

- Heart failure
- Permanent brain damage due to lack of oxygen
- Pulmonary edema (fluid in the lungs)
- Internal hemorrhage and tissue damage
- Severe burns

#10 Fractures, Dislocations and Sprains

Causes

Most fractures are caused by some form of trauma or disease.

- Motor vehicle accidents
- Severe blows or twists
- Jumping or falling (cats frequently fall from high-rise apartments)
- Excessive muscular contractions (strenuous muscle exertion, electrocution)
- Some bone disease such as nutritional imbalance and cancer

Definitions

- *Closed Fracture* — The skin or mucus membranes have not been penetrated by the bone ends
- *Open Fracture* — The skin or mucus membranes have been punctured or torn by the bone ends
- *Dislocations* — A displacement of one or more bones that enter into the formation of a joint so the joint surfaces are no longer in proper contact
- *Sprain* — The partial tearing or stretching of the ligaments around the joint

GENERAL INJURIES

Signs

Rarely will all of the following signs be present at the same time.

- Inability to use a leg. This lack of use can be either partial or complete. **NOTE** — A fractured leg usually will not bear weight
- Pain, especially at or near the injury site
- Abnormal mobility and angulation (A leg may dangle or movement may be noted at the site of the injury)
- Swelling and discoloration (bruising)
- Grating or crepitus (A sound that can be heard when the ends of a broken bone rub together)
- Protruding bone fragments can be seen through the skin
- Shortening of the limb may occur

Treatment

The object of treatment is to prevent further injury, reduce the amount of pain present, stop hemorrhage and prevent infection.

IMPORTANT — Do not try to reset a fracture or clean associated wounds. Handle the injured area as little as possible.

- Use proper restraint such as applying a mouth tie for dogs and wrapping a cat in a blanket. (See Section #35 — Restraint/Transportation). **NOTE** — These animals are usually in severe pain and will bite

- Potential spinal injuries should have the back, head and forelegs stabilized while transporting to a hospital. Create an emergency stretcher by tying or taping an animal to a board, piece of cardboard or other rigid structure. A blanket pulled taut by at least three people is a second choice (See Section #35 — Restraint/Transportation)
- Control hemorrhage with pressure bandages (Do not use a tourniquet)
- Treat shock (See Section #26 — Shock)
- Protect open fractures with a sterile dressing
- Apply a temporary splint, if possible. Do not bandage fractures of the pelvic area, shoulder blade, rib cage or upper limbs. Apply a Modified Robert Jones Bandage or a regular homemade splint (See Section #16 — Bandaging/Splints/Collars)
- When excessive struggling makes the application of a splint very difficult or impossible, transport the animal directly to a veterinarian, unless you are several hours away

SPINAL INJURIES

Signs

- Paralysis may be present
- Head may be thrust backward
- The forelegs may be stiff and rigid

Treatment

See treatment for general injuries page 61.

Complications

- Bone infection
- Permanent nerve damage and paralysis

HEAD INJURIES

Signs

- Decreased alertness
- Incoordination
- Unconscious
- Convulsions
- Unequal pupil size (black central portion of eyes are not of equal size)
- Colorless fluid or blood coming from ears or nose
- Vomiting

Treatment

See treatment for general injuries.

Complications

- Brain hemorrhage and edema
- Eye and ear injuries
- Permanent brain damage

References: 1, 12, 13, 17, 23, 25

#11 Allergic Reactions

ANAPHYLACTIC SHOCK

Definition

A potentially fatal, acute, generalized reaction (anaphylaxis) caused by hypersensitivity in the body to certain foreign materials or drugs. Examples are insect stings, inhaled pollens or other materials, and certain foods.

NOTE — Animals may go into shock within 1 to 15 minutes after contacting the offending substance. Death can occur rapidly, but fortunately anaphylactic shock is not common in small animals.

Signs

Dogs

11.

- Restlessness
- Local swelling (insect bites)
- Vomiting
- Diarrhea
- Shock
- Collapse

Cats

- Salivation
- Difficult breathing (major sign which differs between dogs and cats)
- Local swelling (insect bites)
- Vomiting

- Shock
- Incoordination
- Collapse

Treatment

- An injection of epinephrine should be given immediately by a veterinarian
- Establish a clear air way and give oxygen, if available
- Give cardiopulmonary resuscitation (See Section #4 — Cardiac Arrest)
- Treat for shock (See Section #26 — Shock)

HIVES/MUZZLE SWELLING

Synonyms

Urticaria, angioneurotic edema

Causes

- Insect bites
- Contact with chemicals
- Foods (meals, prepared dog foods, garbage)
- Drugs (penicillin, etc.)

Signs

- Swellings develop within 10-30 minutes from an insect bite or from an ingested drug within several hours
- Skin plaques or swelling of the face, head, lips, ears, genitalia or surface of the body
- Eyelids may close because of swelling

- Rubbing the mouth and eyes along the ground or with the paws
- Vomiting and/or diarrhea. **NOTE** — This type of allergic reaction can be alarming to the owner, but rarely causes serious injury to the pet. An exception is severe respiratory distress in which case veterinary assistance should be obtained immediately.

Localized infections (cellulitis) and abscesses are conditions that are frequently confused with these allergic reactions.

Treatment

- Wash the animal free of any chemical residues or other materials
- Cold packs or baking soda pastes may be applied to individual insect bites
- When respiratory distress is present, administer oral antihistamines. A normal human adult does may be used for dogs over 60 lbs
- Give artificial respiration, if needed. (See Section #4)
- Administer oxygen, if available
- Treat for shock as indicated (See Section #26—Shock)
- When ingestion of the causative agent is suspected, give a laxative of milk of magnesia and an enema (See Section #13—Constipation)
- Seek veterinary assistance. Telephone ahead so the hospital will be prepared for your arrival

Complications

- Anaphylaxis
- Severe bacterial infections

SKIN ALLERGIES

Causes

- Allergic atopic dermatitis is a skin inflammation resulting from a hypersensitivity to common allergens. Examples of causative substances are pollens from grasses and weeds, trees, house dust, feathers, wool, molds, insect bites (especially fleas), stings, injections and some foods
- Allergic contact dermatitis is an inflammation of the skin which results from direct contact with some substances. Examples of such substances are dichlorvos flea collars, poison oak or ivy, stinging nettles, wool or nylon carpeting, soaps and insecticides

Signs

- Frequent scratching
- Biting and licking of feet, legs, abdomen (chronic licking changes hair to reddish-brown)
- Reddening of the skin
- Tender and infected skin areas ("hot spots")
- Face or ear rubbing
- Watery nasal discharge and sneezing
- Excessive tearing and conjunctivitis

Treatment

- Prevent self-mutilation (See Section #16 — Bandaging/Splints/Collars)
- Eliminate any external parasites, especially fleas
- Bathe the area with a mild shampoo — rinse and dry well
- Consult a veterinarian

NOTE — Allergies left untreated can become badly infected

Complications

- Self-mutilation
- Severe skin infections

Prevention

- Frequent bathing (every 2 to 3 weeks)

References: 17, 18

Notes

#12 Appetite Loss

APPETITE

Synonyms

Anorexia, inappetence

Signs

- Absence of or decrease in food consumption

Causes

Normal Behavior Changes

- Being frightened or excited
- Recent environment change (traveling, moving)
- Being in season (estrus) or a female nearby being in season
- Having a birth recently

Diet Variables

- Change in diet
- Feeding inconsistent amounts of food
- Overeating

Illness

- Fever
- Gastrointestinal upset or obstruction
- Specific diseases

Trauma

- Pain resulting from injury
- Painful conditions of the teeth, mouth and throat

You should not be concerned if an occasional meal is missed. If an animal does not eat, simply pick up its food and feed it again at the next meal.

Your pet's food consumption should be fairly consistent. The following loss of appetite is not unusual:

AGE OF ANIMAL	DURATION OF APPETITE LOSS
1 - 2 months	8 hrs.
2 - 3 months	12 hrs.
3 - 4 months	16 hrs.
Adult	24 hrs.

Refusal to eat for longer periods of time may indicate a problem. The temperature should be taken and the animal examined for other symptoms. (See Section #29 - Fever) Be particularly observant of such things as coughing, vomiting and diarrhea.

Consult a veterinarian after:

- 24 hours when other symptoms accompany a change or loss of appetite
- 36 hours when there has been no intake of foot or water
- 72 hours when there has been a change in appetite and no other symptoms are present. IMPORTANT NOTE - A complete loss of appetite need not occur, but merely a change in appetite may be significant.

Treatment

- Give lesser amounts of food, but feed more frequently
- Do not make food available for more than a l0 minute period
- Change temporarily to a very enticing food. Use something with a pungent odor such as liverwurst or tuna fish

#13 Constipation

Definition

- Constipation is the occurrence of infrequent or difficult passage of feces. A synonym is intestinal impaction

Causes

Dietary, Ingestion of

- Bones
- Undigestable materials such as hair
- Large quantities of dry food without adequate water intake
- Insufficient bulk (mainly meat diets with very little dry food or cereal products)

Painful Defecation

- Impacted or infected anal glands
- Anal lesions
- Traumatic pelvic injuries

Mechanical

- Hair matted around anus
- Healed pelvic fractures
- Enlarged prostate gland
- Internal parasite masses
- Tumors

Neurological Disorders

- Loss of intestinal muscle tone in older animals
- Spinal or pelvic injuries

Other

- Suppressed defecation due to kenneling
- Lack of exercise

Signs

- Straining with unsuccessful attempt to defecate
- Pain associated with attempts to defecate
- Dry and hard bowel movements
- Passing small quantities of fluid only (often confused with diarrhea)
- Blood streaked feces
- Impacted material in the rectum
- Vomiting
- Weakness of the hind legs

IMPORTANT - A male cat's straining may be due to a urethral obstruction and can prove fatal if not treated within a few hours. (See Section #32 - Urethral Obstruction)

NOTE - Constipation is often mistaken for other serious problems which can be aggravated by the use of laxatives. Excessive straining that occurs following diarrhea and a urethral obstruction in a male cat or dog are the most commonly confused conditions. Never give a laxative if you have any reason to suspect your pet may have swallowed a ball, toy or other object.

Treatment (Use one of the following)

Enema (Dogs only) - Use warm water or a pediatric disposable enema. Insert the tip of the enema gently into the rectum and give 1 ounce per 10 lbs. of body weight.

- Suppositories - Use a children's suppository and follow the indicated dosage according to body weight. Insert the suppository gently into the rectum and hold in place for 4 to 5 minutes.
- Lubricating Agent - Mineral Oil - place I teaspoon per I0 lbs. of body weight directly in the food. IMPORTANT-Improper oral administration can result in fatal pneumonia. Do not administer mineral oil except by placing it in the food.
- Milk of Magnesia - For dogs give I teaspoon orally for every 8 lbs. of body weight
- White petroleum jelly - for cats apply ½ teaspoon for each 10 lbs. of body weight, directly in the mouth or on the upper lip (See Section #18—Medication Administration)
- Consult a veterinarian whenever the condition is not resolved or tends to persist

NOTES

#14 Coughing

Definition

A cough is a reflex response to some form of irritation of the lining of the respiratory tract. A cough is frequently a symptom of a specific disease and not a separate or isolated entity.

Causes (Normal)

- Exercise
- Excitement
- Change in air temperature
- Excessive pulling on a leash
- Drinking water rapidly

Causes (Abnormal)

- Respiratory tract infections, such as bronchitis and pneumonia
- Infectious diseases
- Heart disease
- Chest injuries
- Hairballs (accumulation of hair in the stomach of cats)
- Parasitic diseases
- Heartworm infestation
- Foreign body in the throat
- Smoke or chemical inhalation
- Allergy
- Thoracic tumors

Consult a veterinarian when there is

- Frequent coughing

NOTE - Coughing 2 to 3 times a day is normal. Coughing 2 to 3 times an hour is not normal.

- Coughing that persists for more than 24 hours
- Fever (See Section #29 - Fever)
- Difficult, noisy or open mouth breathing
- Discharge from the nose and/or eyes
- Blue lips and tongue (See illustration page 127)
- Animal tires easily
- Frothy, bright red blood is coughed up
- Depression or lack of appetite

Treatment

- Use a regular human cough syrup (Give according to directions on a weight basis)

NOTE - Use only for a dry, harsh sounding, non-productive cough. Do not use for more than a few hours without specific instructions from a veterinarian.

- Consult a veterinarian if coughing persists

Prevention

- Avoid abrupt or extreme temperature changes
- Prevent excessive pulling when on a leash
- Eliminate exposure to air pollutants such as smoke, dust, fumes and chemicals

#15 Diarrhea

Definition

Diarrhea is the frequent passage of unformed, abnormally soft or fluid stools. It is not a specific diagnosis, but rather a symptom of an intestinal disorder or underlying disease process.

Causes

Dietary

- Changes in regular diet
- Overeating
- Ingestion of spoiled or unusual foods

Emotional Stress

- Excitement or fear
- Pain

Parasites (Intestinal)

Specific Diseases

- Intestinal disease
- Generalized or metabolic disease
- Poisons

Do not be concerned if your dog or cat has an occasional soft stool. When this occurs, reduce the food consumption and continue to observe the nature of the stool. Your pet's bowel movements should be fairly consistent.Consult a veterinarian after

- 24 hours in very young animals or when other signs accompany diarrhea or blood is present
- 48 hours when diarrhea persists or reoccurs
- 72 hours when an unusual stool consistency exists, but severe diarrhea is not present. NOTE - A mere change in stool consistency may be significant, even though definite diarrhea is absent.

Observations as to the nature of normal stools

- Frequency - Adults - I to 2 times per day; puppies or kittens - 2 to 5 times per day
- Quantity - Should be consistent but varies with the type of food fed
- Color - Light to dark brown, but varies with the type of food fed
- Consistent - Formed
- Odor - Minimal
- Blood - Absence
- Mucus - Absence

IMPORTANT - When the animal's condition warrants seeking professional help, take along a recent stool sample for examination.NOTE - Flatulence or gas frequently results from some abnormality in digestion. The most common causes are consumption of high protein diets (especially meat), spoiled food or large quantities of food.

Treatment

Treating diarrhea immediately will assist in an early recovery and may prevent serious complications. The goal of treatment is to eliminate the cause and restore a normal condition as soon as possible.

Food

- Withhold all food; weaned puppies and kittens 6-8 hours; adults 24 hours
- Feed a soft bland diet - make home prepared food or obtain a prescription diet food from a veterinarian

Home Prepared Bland Diet

Mix 1/2 cup cottage cheese or boiled hamburger or boiled chicken with 1/2 cup boiled white rice.

Feeding Instructions:

Give a quantity approximately 1/2 of your pet's normal food consumption for one day. Divide into small amounts to feed 3 to 4 times daily. Reintroduce normal diet gradually over 3 to 4 feedings.

NOTE - Pay particular attention to any bowel movements during the next few days. Do not return to a normal diet until the stools are normal.

Water

- Withhold all water for 6 - 8 hours
- Reintroduce water slowly
- Small breeds of dogs and cats - 1/3 cup every hour

- Medium size dogs - 1/2 cup every hour
- Large dogs - I cup every hour

Medication

- Treat with an intestinal protective (Pepto-Bismol or Kaopectate), administer orally, 1 tablespoon (15ml) per 20 lbs. of body weight every 2-6 hours.
- A sore anal area may result from diarrhea and may be soothed by applying Vaseline or a hemorrhoidal preparation several times a day.
- Consult a veterinarian, if condition exists for more than 36-48 hours.

Prevention

- Avoid sudden change in the amounts or types of food
- Do not permit a pet to roam or run free. This will eliminate access to decomposed foods.
- Avoid placing undue emotional stress on your pet
- Have your pet examined routinely for intestinal parasites

Regular Homemade Splints (see illustration)

The splint should be firm and of adequate length to keep the joints immobilized above and below the fracture.

- Wrap the leg with cotton or cloth padding
- Apply flat boards, magazines or something similar on the outside
- Tape or tie with strips of cloth or a handkerchief

REGULAR HOMEMADE SPLINTS

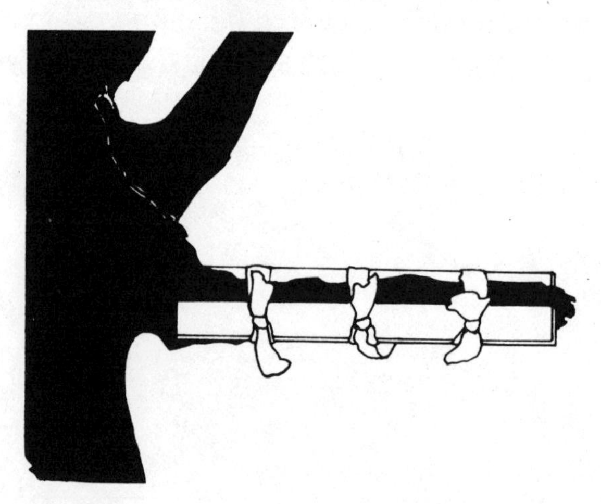

Modified Robert Jones Bandage (see illustrations)

This bandage is bulky but gives good support without interfering with circulation.

- Apply a sterile dressing to any wounds and cover the leg with a roll of gauze.
- Apply several wraps of roll cotton uniformly around the leg. Use less cotton on small dogs or cats.
- Compress the cotton with a roll of gauze.
- Apply a firm layer of an elastic bandage (Ace) or stretch adhesive tape (Elastikon).
- Tape the bandage in place

MODIFIED ROBERT JONES
BANDAGE APPLICATION

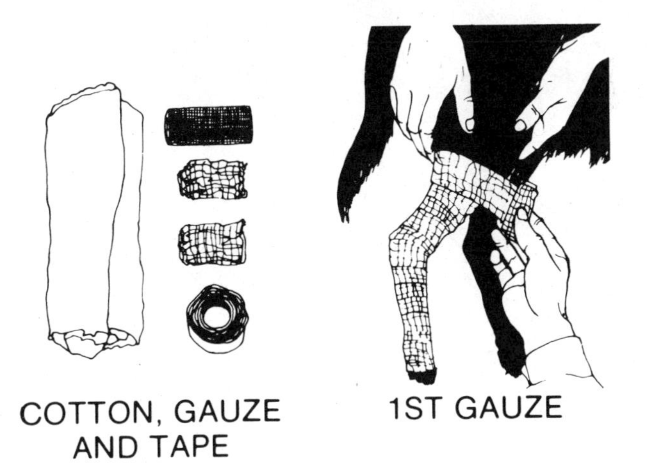

COTTON, GAUZE AND TAPE

1ST GAUZE

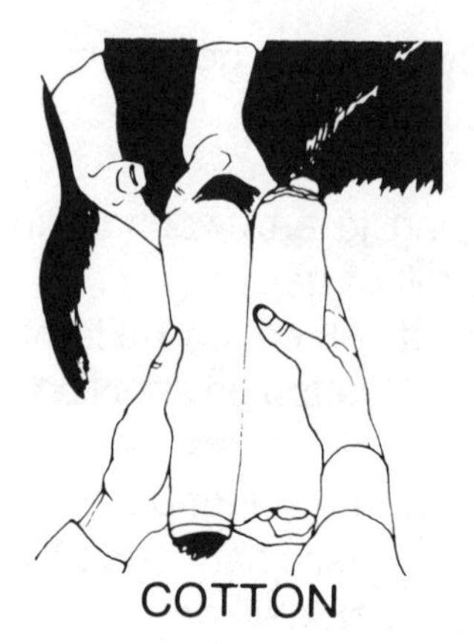

COTTON

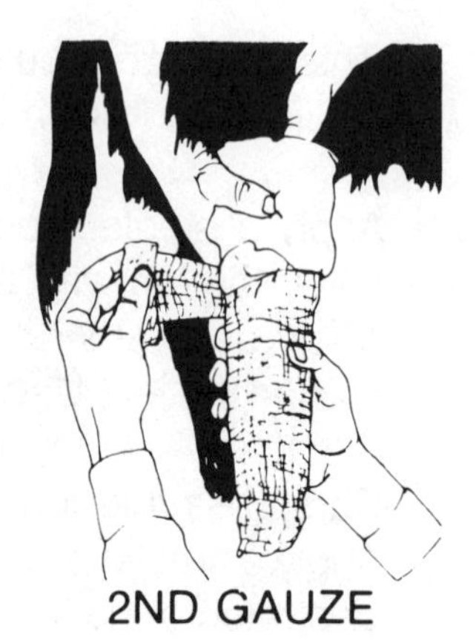

2ND GAUZE

ELASTIC
BANDAGE

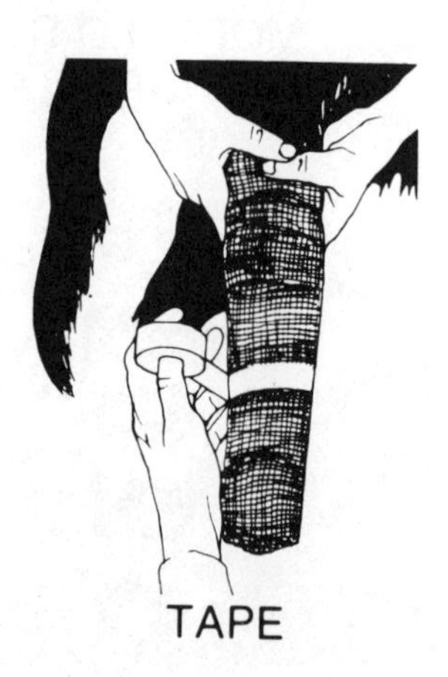

TAPE

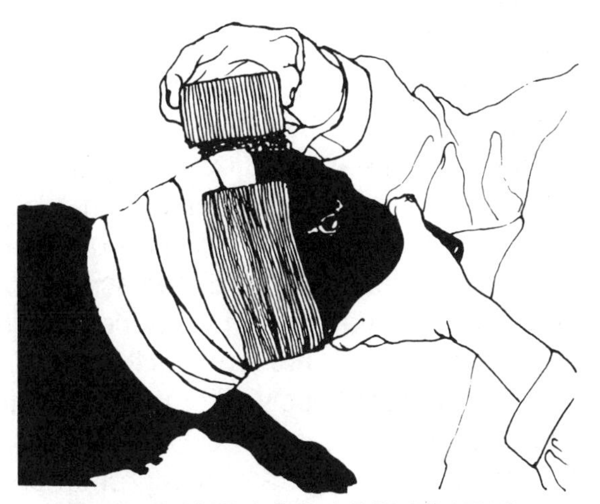

HEAD BANDAGE APPLICATION

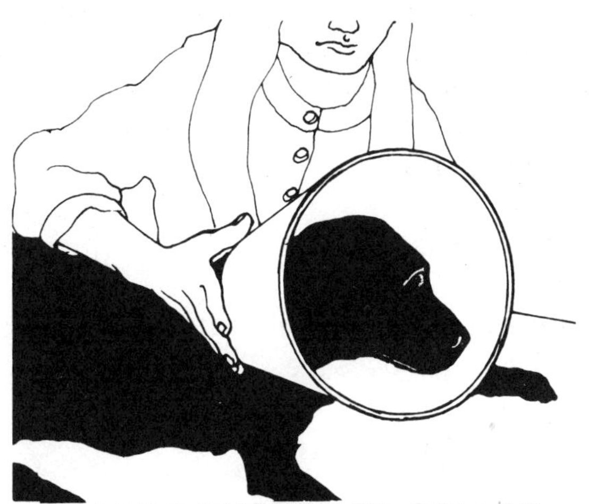

PLASTIC BUCKET OR COLLAR

#17 Grooming/Removal of Stains/Odor/Etc.

Removal of Tar, Asphalt or Chewing Gum

- When a large area is involved clip the hair off in the involved area and wash the skin with soap and water
- When a small area is involved the material should be allowed to harden and then cut off. Chewing gum can be hardened by applying ice cubes directly to it and then scraping it off when it is brittle enough. The ice should be applied only to the hair and not the skin. Ether can be used cautiously to remove the material from small areas.
- Materials over large areas can often be softened by soaking in mineral or vegetable oil for 24 hours. Bandaging the area with oil may be helpful. The tar or asphalt should then be washed repeatedly with soap and water.
- Very few grease solvents are safe to use.

Removal of Paint

Water Base Paint

- Wash repeatedly with warm water and soap as soon as possible

Oil Base Paint

- Treat paint soaked hair promptly
- Fresh paint should be wiped off with dry cloths and then washed with warm water and soap
- Dried paint should be cut off with blunt scissors and the remaining hair washed several

times with warm water and soap

- Difficult patches of paint can have rubbing alcohol or Borax applied and rubbed off with a dry cloth. IMPORTANT - Do not use paint removers, kerosene, turpentine or gasoline since they can severely irritate the skin. Determine if any paint may have been swallowed (See Section #24 - Poisons).

Removal of Skunk Odor

- When skunk spray causes irritation of the eyes, flush them with water (See Section #8—Ear/Eye Injuries) and apply a mild eye ointment (Boric acid ointment) or a few drops of olive oil.
- Wash the animal repeatedly with water and a gentle shampoo or soap.
- Soak the entire animal with tomato juice or concentrated citrus juice for 10 minutes or more and then rinse off thoroughly. The odor, caused by a chemical named mercaptan, can be neutralized by any kind of inexpensive household source of Vitamin C.

STAIN REMOVAL

Removing Blood

Washables

- Soak the stain in cold water, never hot water, until it turns light brown then wash in warm soapy water
- A persistent stain may be soaked in plain non-sudsing household ammonia and water (Add two tablespoons per gallon of water). Rinse

thoroughly. Test colored fabrics for color fastness before soaking
- A mild bleach treatment can be used

Non-Washables

- Soak the stain in cold water. Never use hot water
- A mild bleach treatment can be used provided the dye can withstand it, if not dry the fabric in the sun. This will help bleach the stain

Removing Urine and Vomitus

Urine and vomitus are usually acidic secretions and cause a bleaching effect rather than staining. Prompt cleaning is important for colored items.

Colored Rugs or Fabrics

- Blot as much urine as possible. Use absorbent paper materials such as paper towels, napkins or tissues. Discard the paper as it becomes moist and continue blotting until the fabric feels damp but not wet
- Sponge the fabric thoroughly with cool water and blot again. Repeat the process
- When the fabric's color seems faded, sponge the stain as soon as possible with a solution of two tablespoons of plain non-sudsing household ammonia and one cup of water. The ammonia counteracts the effect of the acid, but may affect the color.
- If the color is not restored at this point sponge the area with white vinegar. Use cool water

and rinse well. NOTE - The dye in the fabric has probably been destroyed if the above is not successful. Check with a dry cleaner for help in restoring the color.

White Rugs or Fabrics

- Sponge the spot with cool water or soak if it is washable fabric
- Rub in a mild to strong detergent, depending on the delicacy of the fabric and the stubbornness of the stain. A small area should be tested first.

Washable

- Apply a liquid detergent and rub in lightly with the edge of a large spoon
- Rinse and wash the area well

Non-Washable

- Mix 1 teaspoon of mild detergent and I teaspoon of white vinegar in I quart of warm water. Work a small amount of this cleaning solution into the soiled area
- Blot any excess liquid from the area

Urine Odor Removal

A faint remnant of the odor is easily left which may re-attract your pet to the same area. Three things can be done to discourage this:

- The soiled area must be cleaned - not only the carpet itself, but also the pad underneath it as well as the flooring. Failure to do this will consistently leave a faint trace of odor

- Commercial odor removing or masking products are available. White vinegar, weakly diluted with water, is also helpful
- Pets can be discouraged from returning to the area by applying small amounts of cologne or commercial repellents to the spots. Restricting pets from the involved area for several weeks is another alternative

Removing Fecal Material

- Remove the feces from the soiled area as soon as possible and wipe up any liquid
- Moisten the area thoroughly with cool water
- Non-Washables - Mix 1/2 teaspoon of mild detergent and 1 teaspoon of white vinegar in1 quart of warm water. Work a small amount of this solution into the soiled area and blot

Reference: 9

Notes

#18 Medication Administration

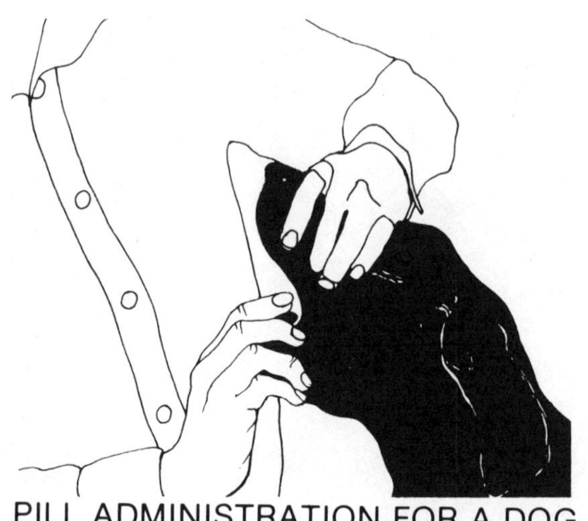

PILL ADMINISTRATION FOR A DOG

PILL ADMINISTRATION FOR A CAT

OINTMENT ADMINISTRATION TO A CAT

APPLYING OINTMENT TO A CAT'S EYE

No.	Topic	Category
1.	Abdominal Distension	ACCIDENTS AND INJURIES
2.	Bleeding	
3.	Burns/Smoke Inhalation	
4.	Cardiac Arrest / Cardio-pulmonary Resuscitation	
5.	Choking	
6.	Convulsions	
7.	Drowning/Artificial Respiration	
8.	Ear/Eye Injuries	
9.	Electrical Shock	
10.	Fractures/Dislocations/Sprains	
11.	Allergic Reactions	ILLNESS AND DISEASE
12.	Appetite Loss	
13.	Constipation	
14.	Coughing	
15.	Diarrhea	
16.	Bandaging/Splints/Collars	GENERAL
17.	Grooming/Removal of Stains/Odor/Etc.	
18.	Medication Administration	

#19 Foreign Bodies

FISH HOOKS

Deeply embedded fish hooks often require a general anesthetic prior to their removal.

IMPORTANT - Fish hooks that are close to the eyes should never be removed. This should be done only by a veterinarian. Do not pull backwards on a hook with a buried barb.

Treatment

- Gently withdraw the hook if the barbed portion has not penetrated the skin
- Push the hook forward until the barb protrudes through the skin. Cut the shank of the hook with a cutting tool (sidecutters or pliers work well) and remove
- Apply pressure around the wound to cause bleeding, clean thoroughly, and, if required apply a bandage
- Treat with antibiotics, especially if swelling and redness of the tissues occurs.

PORCUPINE QUILLS

An emergency may exist following an encounter with a porcupine. The outcome often depends upon the number and location of the quills and the pet's temperament. Many animals handle a limited number of quills with little discomfort while others approach hysteria. Quills in the neck, shoulders and legs migrate and may break off easily, indicating the need for immediate attention.

Signs

- Visible quills
- Discomfort indicated by frantic pawing at the quills, especially if in the mouth

Treatment

- A general anesthetic given by a veterinarian is usually required before they are removed.
- A few quills can often be removed without sedation. Grasp the quill firmly near the skin with pliers and slowly pull straight out.
- Wipe the wounds with an antiseptic. NOTE - Quills tend to break off if jerked or pulled out at an angle. The location of a quill broken off beneath the skin should be noted for further treatment.

Fallacies

- It is not valid to assume that cutting off the ends of the quills before pulling, twisting the quills or pouring vinegar over them will aid in their removal.
- It is not valid to assume that quill removal without anesthesia will teach your pet not to repeat the encounter. NOTE - If a dog attacks a porcupine more than once, it should be assumed that he will again if the opportunity presents itself.

Prevention

- If your pet encounters a porcupine, restrain him immediately
- Do not let your pet run free without supervision in areas known to be inhabited by porcupines.

FOXTAILS (Plant Awns and Seeds)

Ears/Eyes (See Section #8 - Ear/Eye Injuries)

Nose

Signs

- Recurring violent sneezing
- Nasal discharge (bloody, blood-specked or cloudy) - note the side on which the discharge occurs

Treatment

- Try to gently pull out a visible foreign body
- Seek veterinary assistance

Feet, Toes and Other Areas

Signs

- Chewing or licking at the area
- Lameness
- Draining wounds or abscesses
- Pain and swelling
- Bleeding

Treatment

- Try to gently pull out a visible foreign body
- Seek veterinary assistance
- Gently squeezing may sometimes expel the foreign body

- Treat with antibiotic ointment following removal
- Soak affected part in warm water
- Seek veterinary assistance

Prevention

- Perform a daily examination, especially in long haired animals that spend considerable time outside

FOREIGN OBJECT INGESTION

Mouth (See Section #5 - Choking)
Stomach/Intestine (bones, balls, sticks, stones, hairballs and threaded needles)

Signs

- Persistent vomiting
- Poor appetite
- Abdominal pain
- Diarrhea

Treatment

- Withhold food and water
- Consult a veterinarian

NOTE - A string or thread hanging from the mouth or rectum should not be pulled out. Thread attached to a needle should have its ends tied together to prevent unthreading until veterinary assistance is obtained.

#20 Frostbite/Cold Exposure

FROSTBITE

Freezing of tissue usually occurs in the peripheral parts of the body which are sparsely covered with hair and where circulation of blood is poor. In cats frostbite occurs most frequently on the tips of the ears and the tail. In dogs the scrotum, ears, feet, teats, and tail are the most commonly affected areas. Animals caught in traps during the winter are susceptible to frostbite.

NOTE - Animals that are well fed and conditioned to cold temperatures can survive severe conditions if sheltered from wind and moisture.

Signs

- Flushed and reddened tissues
- White or greyish tissues
- Evidence of shock
- Scaliness of the skin
- Possible sloughing of surface tissue

IMPORTANT - Do not rub or massage frozen tissues. Never apply snow or ice. Tissue damage is greatly increased if thawing is followed by refreezing.

Treatment

- Prevent further contact with snow or cold
- Prevent self-mutilation of the area
- Warm the affected area rapidly by immersing in warm water (102-105° F); or use warm

moist towels that are changed frequently. Discontinue warming as soon as the affected tissues become flushed.
- Gently dry the affected tissues, lightly wrap in a clean, dry bandage, and protect from further injury
- Seek veterinary assistance

NOTE - If the tissues are known to have been thawed and refrozen, warm at room temperature only (70-74°).

COLD EXPOSURE

Freezing and hypothermia are more likely to occur from exposure to very cold temperatures, high humidity, wind or immersion in water. Hypothermia is a reduced or lowered body temperature. Animals that are young, injured, ill, starving or fatigued are more susceptible.

Signs

- Shivering
- Numbness
- Low body temperature (rectal temperature below 94°F)
- Drowsiness
- Marked muscular weakness
- Decreased pulse and respiratory rate
- Frozen extremities
- Unconsciousness

Treatment

- Prevent further heat loss as soon as possible
- Immerse frozen parts of body in warm water (102°-105° F) NOTE - Do not use hot water
- Cover with warm towels or blankets (An electric blanket may be used)
- Lightly bandage an affected area with a dry, non-adhering bandage
- Raise and lower affected limbs to stimulate circulation
- Treat for shock (See Section #26 - Shock)
- If conscious, give orally a mixture of sugar and warm liquid
- Seek veterinary assistance

Complications

- Shock
- Infection
- Tissue destruction

References: 1, 15

Notes

#21 Heat Stroke

Synonyms

Hyperthermia, sunstroke, heat stress and heat prostration or exhaustion

Causes

- Confinement in a closed area or automobile that is exposed to the sun and has poor ventilation
- Excessive exercise and/or excitement
- Increased humidity and poor ventilation
- Unavailability of drinking water
- Partially obstructed airways in normal animals, i.e. Brachycephalic (short-headed) breeds of dogs

NOTE - A long haired animal's coat insulates the animal against the heat as well as the cold. Clipping the hair off will not prevent heat stroke, but in fact, may increase the likelihood of its occurrence.

Signs

- Extreme panting
- Difficult breathing
- Disorientation and weakness
- Salivation
- Vomiting
- Diarrhea
- Rapid pulse
- High body temperature (105-110°F rectally)
- Bright red gums
- Cyanosis or blue lips and tongue (See illustration page 127)

- Shock
- Sudden collapse

Treatment

21.

- Place in a cool or shaded area
- Lower the animal's temperature by submerging it in cold water or spraying with a hose
- Take the animal's temperature rectally every 5 minutes until it reaches 103.5°F. Avoid overcooling
- If its temperature remains above 103.5° F for l0 to l5 minutes, give a cold water enema
- The animal should be dried and encouraged to drink when it feels better
- If symptoms of shock are present, treat accordingly (See Section #26 - Shock)

IMPORTANT - Do not cool the animal's body below 103.5°F, as its temperature will continue to drop and hypothermia (abnormally low body temperature) may result.

Prevention

- Animals left outside during hot days should be provided with a shaded area and cool fresh water
- During hot weather strenuous exercise should be limited to early mornings and evenings
- Maintain a proper body weight for your pet's size and age

Complications

- Brain damage
- Secondary infections

References: 1, 3, 14

#22 Insect Bites/Stings

BEES, HORNETS, WASPS

Stings usually occur in the mouth or on the nose or feet.

Signs

- Pain
- Evidence of scratching, licking or rubbing the head on the ground
- Swelling
- Presence of a stinger (bees only)
- Excessive salivation, if the sting is inside the mouth

Treatment

- Removal of the stinger with forceps
- Wasp stings are alkaline and can be neutralized with vinegar or lemon juice
- Bee stings are acid and are neutralized by baking soda
- Cold pack application
- Apply calamine or an antihistamine cream

Complications

- Stings on the tongue or in the mouth of Brachycephalic (short-headed) dogs such as Boxers, Bulldogs and Pugs may cause swelling and result in difficult breathing. Asphyxiation and death may occur.IMPORTANT - Seek veterinary assistance immediately.

- Infection may result from the bite
- Wounds often heal slowly

ANTS, SPIDERS

Ant bites are common in puppies. Spider bites rarely occur.

Signs

- Local pain
- Small circular reddish swellings

Treatment

- Use an antihistamine or corticosteroid cream

Prevention

- Use an insecticide dust or spray on the animal

Complications

- Painful bite
- Infection
- Allergic reactions

FLEAS, LICE, TICKS

Signs

- Itching manifested by scratching, chewing and licking
- Areas of hair loss
- Raw inflamed areas on the skin
- Seeing the parasites

Treatment

- Eliminate external parasites by the use of insecticide shampoos, dusts, sprays or flea collars (use only as directed). Continual preventive treatment is required in many areas of the country
- Obtain prompt veterinary care for uncontrollable scratching. This can lead to self-mutilation and secondary infections
- Removal of ticks consists of applying a small amount of a pet or human insecticide spray, liquid or dust, directly to the area. Do not attempt to detach the tick from the skin for 10 to 15 minutes. Grasp the head at the surface of the skin with tweezers and apply slow, gentle traction. Immediate removal without the use of an insecticide consistently results in leaving the head buried in the skin. This causes increased swelling and infection. Never use gasoline, kerosene or a lighted cigarette to remove a tick. This will cause injury to the skin and usually causes the tick to embed deeper into the skin.

Notes

#23 Mismating/Signs of Estrus

Definition

- Mismating - Accidental or unwanted breeding
- Estrus - The mating period of female animals. The terms “in heat” or “in season” refer to the occurrence of an animal’s estrus. Small breeds of dogs may have their first estrus as early as 6 months of age. Large breeds may be l4 to l6 months of age before they show signs of estrus. Cats frequently have their first estrus shortly before they are 6 months old.

Signs of estrus in dogs

- Swollen vulva
- Vaginal discharge - During the first 5 days of heat (proestrus) the discharge is bloody, during the next 5-9 days the discharge is clear, straw-colored or absent
- Attraction of males
- Receptiveness to males
- Temperament changes are sometimes noted, especially toward other females

Signs of estrus in cats

- Flattening of the back and rolling on the ground
- Elevation of the hind quarters
- Lateral deflection of the tail
- Treading movements with the rear feet
- Voice change with persistent meowing or “calling”

NOTE - These behavior changes precede the acceptance of the male 1 to 2 days

Methods of Pregnancy Termination

- Surgical Neutering. Ovariohysterectomy or "Spaying" - the process of surgically removing the ovaries, fallopian tubes and the uterus. This operation can be performed on an animal that has been accidentally bred from 10 to 14 days after estrus. This method is highly recommended if you do not want your pet to reproduce at a later date. Normally surgical neutering should be done on most female dogs and cats after 6 months of age. Large breeds of dogs may be done at approximately 9 months of age.
- Mismating or Abortion injections - pregnancy can usually be prevented by the administration of an estrogen hormone. Estrogen compounds are used to interfere with the receptivity of the lining of the uterus to accept and maintain a fertilized egg. This method of pregnancy prevention may be performed by a veterinarian within the first 48 hours following breeding. Complications are possible and these should be discussed with the veterinarian. Estrogen therapy for mismating in cats is theoretically possible but rarely used. Many cat owners do not consistently recognize that their pet is in estrus and the majority of matings are not observed.

Complications

Following breeding, the male and female dog may become stuck together or "tied" for some period of time. The male turns around and the dogs remain attached rear to rear. Do not attempt to separate. Injuries can result and separating will not prevent pregnancy. When left alone, they will come apart within l0 to 30 minutes.

Normal Breeding Information

ITEM	DOGS	CATS
Minimum breeding age	7 - 14 months[1]	5 - 12 months
Estrus cycle frequency	Every 4-8 months[2]	Every 15-21 days
Duration of estrus[3]	Usually 10-14 days[4]	4 days, if bred - 7-10 days if not bred
Best breeding time	1st to 3rd days of estrus	1st to 3rd days of estrus
Gestation length	63 days	63-65 days

[1]Varies with breed

[2]Most breeds cycle two times per year

[3]Estrus occurs immediately following vaginal hemorrhage

[4]Dogs should be confined approximately 21 days to prevent breeding

NOTES

#24 Poisons

General

Human error, carelessness and ignorance cause the majority of poison cases. It is very important that the pet owner know the common sources of poisonings. There are frequently no characteristic signs that indicate which specific poison is present or has been ingested.

IMPORTANT - In all cases of poisoning, give first aid and then contact a veterinarian immediately. Bring a sample of the poison to the veterinarian in its original container or a portion of any ingested plant or berry and any vomitus.

Objects of treatment

- Maintain respiration and preserve vital functions
- Dilute the poison
- Remove the poison from the system
- Neutralize with an antidote when possible
- Seek veterinary assistance immediately

Signs

- Excitability
- Lack of coordination
- Convulsions
- Salivation
- Vomiting
- Ulcers on the face and/or paws
- Diarrhea
- Weakness
- Depression
- Pain
- Shock

Treatment

IMPORTANT - If the poison is a strong acid, a strong alkali or a petroleum product such as gasoline or kerosene, do not induce vomiting.

A-Strong Acid (Such as Battery Acid)

- If ingested, dilute with clear liquids such as water or soda pop (Use 1 oz. per 6 lbs. of body weight) NOTE: Avoid giving a weak alkali as the combination of acid and alkali may result in a exothermic reaction and add thermal injury to corrosive injury.
- Irrigate all contaminated areas with copious amounts of water

B-Strong Alkali (Such as Lye)

- If ingested, dilute with clear liquids such as water or soda pop (Use 1 oz. per 6 lbs. of body weight) NOTE: The use of acidic agents (e.g. vinegar, fruit juices) to neutralize the alkali are contraindicated because of the high risk of exothermic burns.
- Irrigate all contaminated areas with copious amounts of water

C-Petroleum Products (such as gasoline or kerosene)

- If ingested, dilute with clear liquids such as water, fruit juices or soda pop (Use 1 oz. per 6 lbs. of body weight)
- Wash exposed areas repeatedly with soap and water, if contact with the skin has occurred

D-Other Poisons (Such as strychnine and poisonous plants)

- If ingested, dilute with milk or clear liquids such as water, fruit juices or soda pop (Use 1 oz. per 6 lbs. of body weight)
- Induce vomiting by one of the following methods:
  - Syrup of Ipecac - Give orally 1 teaspoon per 10 lbs. of body weight but not more than 1 tablespoon should be used with even the largest dog. NOTE - Avoid confusing syrup of ipecac with ipecac fluid extract, which is 14 times stronger
  - Hydrogen Peroxide (3% or less) - Give 1 teaspoon per 10 lbs. or 1 tablespoon per 30 lbs. of body weight orally. This dosage may be repeated once in 10 to 15 minutes, if vomiting does not occur
- Use a specific antidote, if known and available. Follow the directions on the label of the product involved
- Get medical help immediately

E-Absorbed and Contact Poisons (Such as chlorinated hydrocarbons or organophosphates)

- If breathing is absent, check to be sure the air way is open and give artificial respiration (See Section #4 - Cardiac Arrest)
- If a heart beat is absent, give cardiopulmonary resuscitation (See Section #4 - Cardiac Arrest)
- Treat for shock (See Section #26 - Shock)

- Wash thoroughly with soap and water or shampoo. NOTE: Chemical burns should be flushed with water for at least 5 minutes and then treated (See Section #3 - Burns/Smoke Inhalation)
- During excitement or convulsions, protect the animal from injuring itself

F-Inhaled Poisons (Such as carbon monoxide)

- If breathing is absent, check to be sure the airway is open and give artificial respiration (See Section #4 - Cardiac Arrest)
- If a heart beat is absent, give cardiopulmonary resuscitation (See Section #4 - Cardiac Arrest)
- Treat for shock (See Section #26 - Shock)

Considerations with Regard to Inducing Vomiting

- If vomiting has already occurred, further inducement may not be necessary
- Do not administer anything by mouth if the animal is convulsing, depressed, unconscious or has a severely distended abdomen
- Do not induce vomiting if corrosive materials such as a strong acid, alkali or petroleum distillate have been swallowed
- Do not waste time if you have trouble administering first aid, or more than 30 minutes has passed since the poison was ingested. Seek veterinary assistance immediately

Methods of Inducing Vomiting

- Syrup of Ipecac - Give orally 1 teaspoon per 10 lbs. of body weight but not more than 1 tablespoon should be used with even the largest dog. The ipecac should be followed by the administration of water (1 oz. per 6 lbs. of body weight) to increase the volume of stomach contents and vomited material. NOTE - Avoid confusing syrup of ipecac with ipecac fluid extract, which is 14 times stronger
- Hydrogen Peroxide (3% or less) - Give 1 teaspoon per 10 lbs. or 1 tablespoon per 30 lbs. of body weight orally. This dosage may be repeated once in 10 to 15 minutes if vomiting does not occur. IMPORTANT - Take vomitus to the veterinarian

Prevention

- Read labels carefully
- Do not let your pet roam
- Do not permit pets to chew or eat toxic plants. Before you buy a plant, ask if it is known to be toxic to animals or children
- Store all chemicals and medicines in their original containers and in a safe place
- Use snail bait holders which are designed to keep bait away from pets

References: 15, 16, 17, 21, 24, 27, 28

NOTES

#25 Common Poisons, Their Sources and Treatments

Poisons	Common Sources	Treatment*
Acids	Car batteries, metal cleaners	A
Acetaminophen	Aspirin substitutes	D
Alkalis	Cleaning preparations	B
Amphetamine	Diet and stimulant pills	D
ANTU	Rodenticides	D
Arsenic	Herbicides, insecticides	D
Birth control pills	Medicines	D
Bleaches	Cleaning preparations	D
Carbamate	Insecticides—Fire Extinguishers	D-E
Carbon monoxide	Automobile exhausts, space heating equipment	F
Carbon tetrachloride	Cleaning solution, solvents	D
Chlorinated hydrocarbons (Organochlorines)	Insecticides	D-E
Chocolate	Candy, frosting, etc.	D
Cyanide	Herbicides, etc.	D
Detergents	Household items	D
Digitalis	Rodenticides, medicine	D
Ethylene glycol	Antifreeze, heat-exchange fluids, brake and hydraulic fluids	D
Food intoxication	Garbage, etc.	D
Fungicides (many)	Fungicides	D
Herbicides (many)	Herbicides	D
Lead	Paint, linoleum, putty, solder, weights	D
Mace	Animal repellants	E
Metaldehyde	Snail baits, etc.	D
Napthalene	Moth balls or flakes, etc.	D
Organophosphates	Insecticides	D-E
Petroleum products	Gasoline, kerosene, oils, grease, etc.	C

(Continued)

Poisons	Common Sources	Treatment*
Phenols (Cresols)	Cleansers, germicides, wood preservatives	D-E
Phosphorus	Rodenticides, fireworks, matches	D
Pyrethins and pyrethroids	Insecticides	D-E
Rodent poisons (Anticoagulants)	Rodenticides	D
Rotenone	Insecticides	D-E
Salicylate	Aspirin	D
Strychnine	Rodenticides	D
Thallium	Rodenticides	D
Turpentine	Solvent and vehicle	C
Warfarin	Rodenticides	D

*Treatment is keyed to the appropriate letter in Section #24 - Poisons/ General Information.

POTENTIALLY POISONOUS PLANTS

(For treatment, see Section #24 D - Other Poisons, page 116)

COMMON NAME	SCIENTIFIC NAME	TOXIC PORTION
Amaryllis	*Amaryllis sp.*	Bulbs
Apple	*Malus sp.*	Seeds
Apricot	*Prunus armeniaca*	Seeds
Autumn crocus	*Colchicum autumnale*	Bulbs
Azalea	*Rhododendron sp.*	All parts
Black Nightshade	*Solanum nigrum*	Berries
Bleeding heart	*Dicentra sp.*	Foliage, roots
Buttercups	*Ranunculus sp.*	All top growth
Caladium	*Caladium sp.*	Leaf, stem, stalk
Calla lily	*Zantedeschia aethiopica*	Bulbs
Castor bean	*Ricinus communis*	Seed pulp
Cherry	*Prunus sp.*	Seeds
Choke cherry	*Prunus virginianum*	Bark, seeds
Daffodil (Jonquil)	*Narcissus pseudonarcissus*	Bulbs
Daphne	*Daphne sp.*	Bark, leaves, fruit
Dumbcane	*Dieffenbachia, sp.*	All parts
Eggplant	*Solanum sp.*	Green growth, sprouts
Elephant's Ear	*Alocasis antiquorum*	All parts
English Ivy	*Hedera helix*	Berries, leaves
European Bittersweet	*Solanium dulcamara*	Berries
Ficus	*Ficus benjamini*	Leaves
Foxglove	*Digitalis purpurea*	All parts, esp. seeds
Hyacinth	*Hyacinthus orientalis*	Bulbs
Iris	*Iris spp.*	All parts
Japanese Yew	*Taxus cuspidata*	Needles, bark, seeds
Jerusalem Cherry	*Solanium pseudocapsicum*	Berries
Jessamine	*Cestrum sp.*	Flowers, leaves
Jimsonweed	*Datura stramonium*	All parts, esp. seeds
Lantana	*Lantana camara*	Unripe greenish-blue or black berries
Larkspur	*Delphinium sp.*	All parts

(Continued)

COMMON NAME	SCIENTIFIC NAME	TOXIC PORTION
Laurels	*Kalmia sp.*	All parts
Lily of the valley	*Convallaria majalis*	All but ripe fruit
Marijuana	*Cannabis sativa*	All parts
Mescal bean	*Sophora sp.*	Seeds
Mistletoe	*Phoradendron flavescens*	Berries
Monkshood	*Aconitum sp.*	All parts, esp. seeds
Morning Glory	*Ipomea sp.*	Most parts
Mushrooms	*Amanita sp., etc.*	All parts
Oleander	*Nerium oleander*	All parts
Peony	*Paeonia sp.*	Roots
Periwinkle	*Vinca rosea*	Most parts
Peyote	*Lophophora williamsii*	Buttons
Philodendron	*Philodendron sp.*	Leaves, stems, stalks
Poinsettia	*Euphorbia pulcherrima*	All parts, esp. seeds
Poison hemlock	*Conium maculatum*	All parts
Potato	*Solanum tuberosum*	Green growth, sprouts
Precatory beans	*Abrus precatorius*	Seeds
Rhododendron	*Rhododendron sp.*	All parts
Rhubarb	*Rheum rhaponticum*	Leaf blade
Rosary pea (precatory bean)	*Abrus precatorius*	Seeds
Snowdrop	*Galanthus nivalis*	Bulbs
Snow-on-the-Mountain	*Euphorbia sp.*	All parts, esp. seeds
Star-of-Bethlehem	*Ornithogalum umbellatum*	Bulbs
Thornapple	*Datura metaloides*	All parts, esp. seeds
Tobacco	*Nicotiana tobaccum*	All parts
Tomato	*Lycoperscion esculentum*	Green growth, sprouts
Trumpet vine	*Datura arborea*	All parts, esp. seeds
Tulips	*Tulipa sp.*	Bulbs
Water hemlock	*Cicuta maculata*	Mainly tubers
Walnuts	*Juglans sp.*	Hulls
Wisteria	*Wisteria sp.*	Seeds
Yellow oleander	*Thevetia peruviana*	All parts
Yew	*Taxus sp.*	All parts

References 8, 10, 15, 21, 24, 27

#26 Shock

Shock is the failure of the cardiovascular system to provide the body tissues with adequate oxygen.

Causes

- Severe injury
- Blood loss
- Fluid loss (as in vomiting or diarrhea)
- Poisoning
- Infection
- Heart failure
- Obstructions to breathing
- Electrical burns
- Drowning

Signs

- Capillary circulation is poor - refill time is more than 2 seconds (See description and color illustrations page 126)
- Gums and lips are pale in color and dry
- Pulse is weak and rapid (usually over 160 per minute in dogs and 200 per minute in cats)
- Breathing is irregular, shallow and rapid (usually over 40 per minute)
- Pupils are dilated
- Cool feeling to the skin and legs
- Weakness, collapse, or unconsciousness

IMPORTANT - Always treat a seriously injured animal for shock. Shock is aggravated by pain, rough handling or delay in treatment. Do not give the animal anything to eat or drink.

Capillary Refill Time

Roll the animal's lip back and press down on a non-pigmented area of the gums with one finger. This area should turn from pink to almost white in color. Once the pressure is removed, the pink color should return within 1 to 2 seconds. If it takes longer, impaired capillary return is present which is a sign of shock (See color illustrations page 126).

Treatment

- Keep the animal quiet
- Clear the air passages and maintain them free of mucus, blood or vomitus. If breathing has stopped or is slow and irregular, start artificial respiration immediately (See Section #4 - Drowning/Artificial Respiration).
- Control bleeding (See Section #2 - Bleeding)
- If the heart beat stops, give cardiopulmonary resuscitation (See Section #4 - Cardiac Arrest)
- Administer oxygen, if available
- Keep warm. Wrap blankets over and under the animal and place in a warm room or well heated car
- Transport to a veterinary hospital immediately (See Section #35 - Restraint/Transportation). Call ahead so that preparation for your arrival can be made
- Fluids may carefully be given by mouth if medical treatment is not available within two or three hours. Do not give fluids to unconscious, vomiting or convulsing animals. Use a warm water solution of ½ teaspoon table salt and ½ teaspoon baking soda for each quart of water. Administer 1 ounce for each 30 lbs. of body weight every 20-30 minutes for a total of 4 to 5 doses.

CAPILLARY REFILL TIME

See text page 125

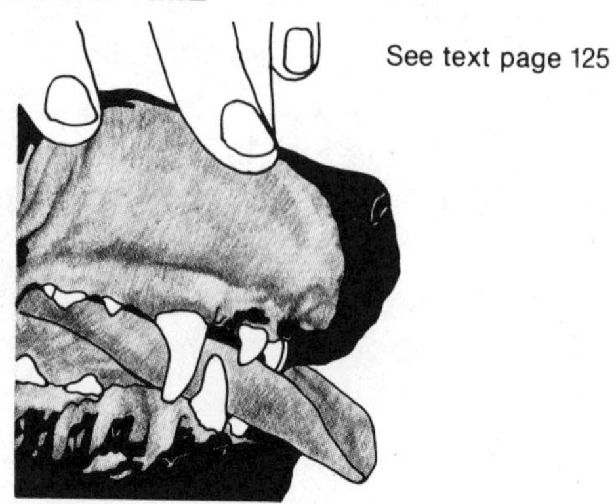

NORMAL PINK COLOR

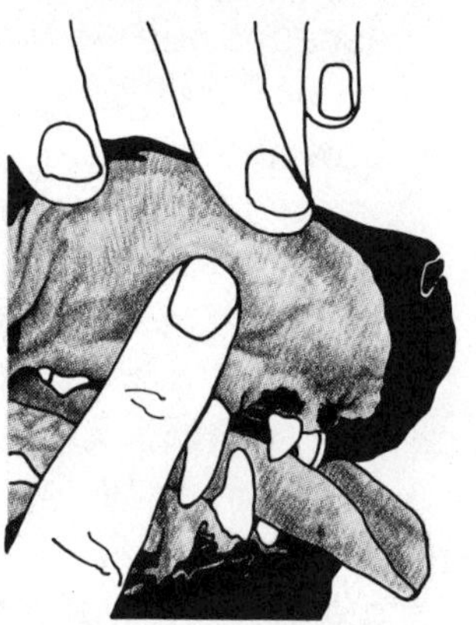

APPLYING PRESSURE TO THE LIP AND GUM

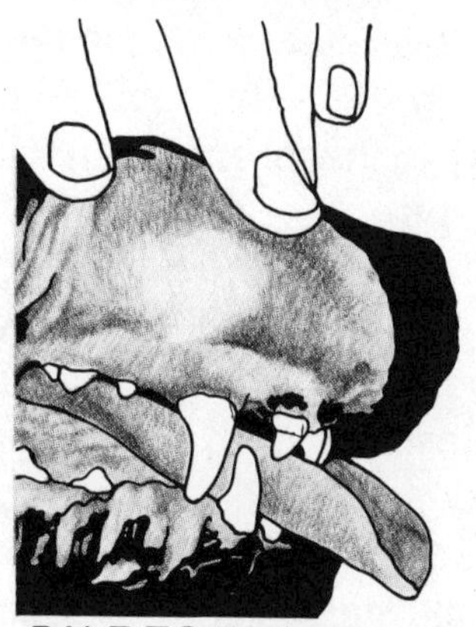

PALE TO WHITE AREA

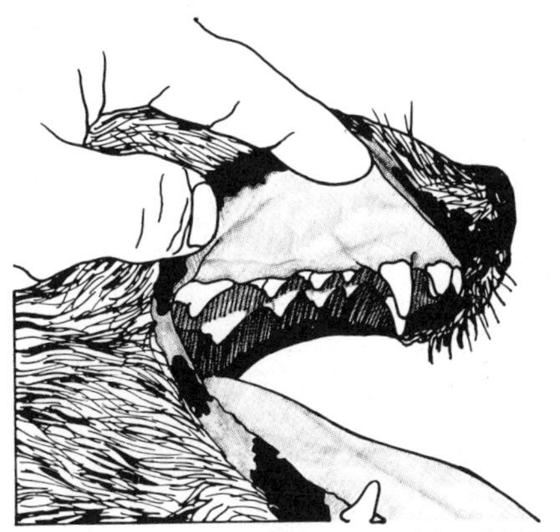

PALE GUMS, LIPS AND TONGUE

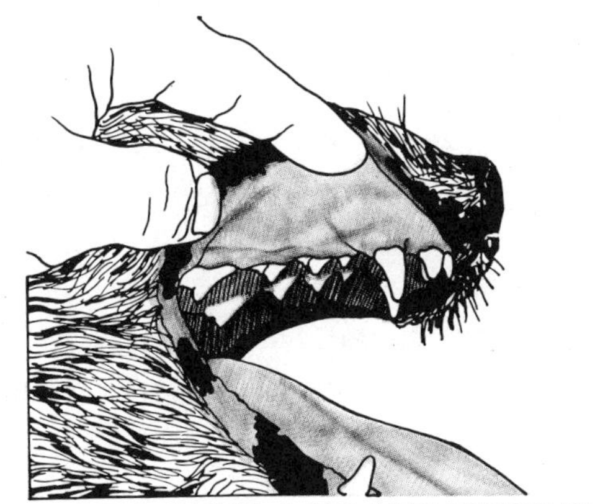

CYANOTIC GUMS, LIPS AND TONGUE

This color is an approximation and is provided as a general guide.

#27 Snakes/Lizards/Toads

SNAKES

Rattlesnakes, copperheads and cotton-mouths are found in the eastern, south-central, midwestern and southwestern United States. Coral snakes are found in the southern United States. The most common place for bites in small animals are the head, shoulder, thighs and legs.

Signs

- Rapid swelling
- Painful area
- Teeth marks
- Discoloration of the skin
- Weakness, rapid pulse, difficult breathing
- Shock

IMPORTANT - If possible, determine if the snake is poisonous. (See illustrations Page131). A dead snake should be brought to the hospital for identification. Avoid crushing the snake's head. Animals, when bitten, may become excited and run. Restraint is essential to prevent the spread of venom.

Treatment

- If seen within 10 minutes and the bite is on a leg, apply a LOOSE 1 inch wide constricting band. This should be placed 2 to 3 inches above the joint above the bite, between the wound and the heart. When properly adjusted there should be some blood oozing from the wound and you should be able to slip a finger under the band. When applied loosely it may be left in place for as long as two hours without removal (DO NOT APPLY TOURNIQUET).

- Treat for shock (See Section #26 - Shock)
- If within 30 minutes of a hospital, immobilize injury and transport immediately without further first aid
- Wash the site of the bite with soap and water and dry
- Apply a clean dressing and bandage
- If available, apply a cold, wet cloth over the wound. Do not pack the wound in ice
- Transport to a veterinarian immediately. Call ahead so that the hospital can be prepared for your arrival
- Nonpoisonous snake bites should be treated as simple puncture wounds

Complications

- Anaphylaxis (See Section #11 - Allergic Reactions)
- Bacterial infections
- Tissue necrosis

LIZARDS

Gila monsters and Mexican beaded lizards are found primarily in the southwestern United States. Venom is injected through their bite. Blue tail lizards are found in the southeastern United States. Cats may be affected if they ingest a portion of a blue tail lizard.

Three species of salamanders (California and European Newts and Unks) are known to have a poisonous effect on dogs and cats.

Signs

- Bite wounds (Gila Monster and Mexican Beaded Lizard)
- Muscular weakness and incoordination
- Vomiting
- Diarrhea
- Shock
- Convulsions
- Paralysis

Treatment

- If still attached, stick an instrument between the jaws and pry loose
- Treat for shock (See Section #26 - Shock)
- Clean and flush wound site with water and a disinfectant
- Transport to a veterinarian immediately

TOADS

There are nine separate species of the bufo toad reported to have caused poisonings in Florida, Hawaii, Texas and other semi-tropical climates. The poisoning results from small animals biting or mouthing the toads.

Signs

- Drooling
- Head shaking
- Rapid heart beat and uncoordinated breathing
- Muscular weakness
- Vomiting

- Diarrhea
- Shock
- Convulsions

Treatment

- Flush the mouth with large amounts of water. Use a hose, if available. If a Blue Tail Lizard has been ingested, induce vomiting (See Page 116).
- If the heart beat stops, give cardiopulmonary resuscitation (See Section #4 - Cardiac Arrest)
- Transport to a veterinary hospital immediately. Call in advance of your arrival so that the hospital will be prepared.

References: 4, 5, 6, 7, 15, 17, 20, 21

IDENTIFYING POISONOUS SNAKES

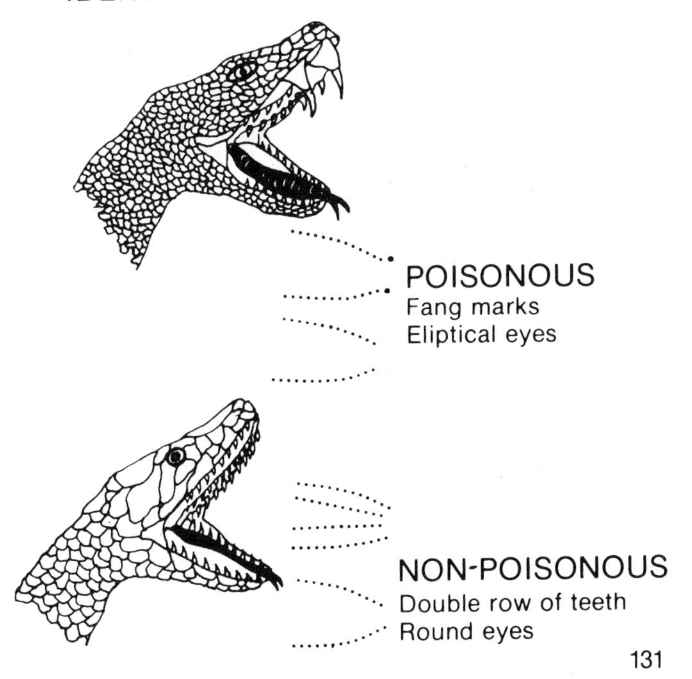

Rattlesnakes are distinguished from the nonpoisonous snakes by their two elongated, canaliculated, upper teeth which can be rotated from their resting position, in which they are folded against the roof of the mouth, to their biting position, where they are almost perpendicular to the upper jaw. The pupils are vertically elliptical but a few nonpoisonous snakes also have such pupils.

Copperheads and cottonmouths have a deep identifiable pit between the eye and the nostril.

Coral snakes two upper teeth are also elongated but they are much shorter than those of the rattlesnakes, and they are fixed. Coral snakes have round pupils, and can be distinguished by their complete rings of black, yellow and red, the red and yellow rings touching.

Identification of the snake on the sole basis of fang or tooth marks is not recommended. Very often copperheads and cottonmouths may strike and leave a single fang puncture wound that is similar to that which might be produced by a nonpoisonous snake.

NOTES

#28 Wounds

Definition

A wound is an injury to tissue or rupture of the skin or mucus membrane due to some type of external force. Wounds are defined as either open or closed. An open wound penetrates the skin, while a closed wound does not.

Types of Open Wounds

- Abrasions and Scratches - These wounds have the outer layers of skin rubbed or scraped off; they are normally caused by falling or glancing blows, or being dragged along the ground. These wounds are usually painful, contaminated with dirt and easily infected
- Incised wounds - These wounds are caused by sharp, cutting instruments such as broken glass and knives. Wound edges are cut cleanly and tend to bleed freely. Quick healing with little or no scar formation is common
- Lacerated wounds - Wounds of this type result from a tearing or bursting force and result in irregular shaped skin edges with considerable underlying tissue damage. Frequent causes include car accidents, bites, bullets and blows from blunt objects. This type of wound results in slow healing, infection and scar formation
- Puncture wounds - The wound is small, but penetrates into the underlying tissue. Pointed instruments such as thorns, nails, bites or bullets are common causes. Bleeding is minimal. However, these wounds tend to be painful and easily become infected.

Treatment of Open Wounds

- Control bleeding by direct pressure or a pressure bandage (See Section #2 - Bleeding)
- Treat for shock (See Section #26 - Shock)
- Prevent further contamination of wounds by bandaging, as indicated, and restrict the animal
- Seek veterinary aid for further examination and treatment. NOTE - When veterinary assistance is immediately available, it is recommended that first aid be limited to the above. If a wound is minor or a veterinarian is not available, additional steps should be taken
- The hair around the wound should be cut or clipped off. Care should be taken to avoid further contamination of the wound
- Clean the wound gently but thoroughly with mild soap and water or a suitable antiseptic solution, such as povidone-iodine (Betadine solution or scrub) NOTE - Hexachlorophene (Phisohex) is toxic in cats and must be avoided
- Apply an antibiotic ointment to the wound
- Apply a clean dressing and bandage if the wound is significant and in a suitable location
- Animals with badly contaminated wounds should receive systemic antibiotics

Types of Closed Wounds

- Contusions or Bruises - In these wounds there is no break in the skin. However, there is soft tissue damage and hemorrhage below the surface. Automobile accidents or blows from blunt objects are frequently the cause

- Hematomas - A hematoma is the accumulation of blood beneath the skin which results in a rounded swelling. The cause is usually trauma that causes blood vessels below the skin to rupture. These wounds are generally not painful

Treatment of Closed Wounds

- Pressure and cold compresses should be applied to fresh wounds or hematomas for 10 to 15 minutes. This will limit pain and swelling
- Prevent further swelling by the application of firm padded bandages
- Hot compresses should be utilized to relieve pain if the swelling has already developed

NOTES

#29 Fever

Definition

- Fever - An elevation of body temperature above the normal range. There is variation in temperature among animals of the same species. An elevated temperature can result from exercise, excitement or high environmental temperatures. Never guess at an animal's temperature by feeling its nose, as this can be very misleading. Take its temperature rectally.
- Normal Temperature for Dogs and Cats (101.5°F±1). A temperature below l00°F or above l03°F is considered abnormal. However, very young animals may have a normal temperature below l00°F.

Treatment

- Always contact a veterinarian first, if possible.
- For a high fever (104-106° F), aspirin may be used (dogs only) to relieve pain and reduce the fever
- Procedure for a very high fever (106°F or above)
  - Lower the animal's temperature by submerging it in cold water or spraying it with a hose
  - Take its temperature rectally every 5 minutes until it reaches 103.5°F. Do not cool below this point as the temperature will continue to drift downward and hypothermia (abnormally low body temperature) may result

- For further treatment (See Section #21 - Heat Stroke)
- Veterinary assistance should be obtained when a fever exists longer than 12 hours

IMPORTANT: Care must be taken with the use of aspirin and acetaminophen in small animals. Dogs and especially cats, can easily die from salicylate poisoning. It is an irritant to the stomach and can cause vomiting and/or ulcers. NEVER GIVE ASPIRIN TO PUPPIES OR CATS. Acetaminophen, a commonly used aspirin substitute, will cause unintentional poisoning if used in cats.

DOGS ONLY

Aspirin Dosage	Frequency	Body Weight
1.5 grains (1 pediatric tablet)	Every 6-8 hours	10 lbs. or less
5.0 grains * (1 regular tablet)	Every 6-8 hours	for each 35 lbs.

*Buffered aspirin is preferred

References: 7, 15, 21, 26

29.

#30 Infections/Abscesses

Definition

- Infection - Invasion of the body by pathogenic microorganisms and the reaction of the tissues to their presence
- Abscess - A localized collection of pus in a cavity formed by the disintegration of tissues

Causes

Wounds

- Bites
- Scratches
- Cuts
- Punctures
- Foreign bodies

Trauma

- Automobile accidents
- Bullets

Signs

Infections (superficial)

- Inflamed skin
- White, yellow or greenish pus around a wound

Infections (deep)

- Fever
- Loss of appetite
- Tenderness
- Heat, redness and swelling of tissues
- Yellow, white or greenish discharge from wounds

Abscesses

- Lack of appetite
- Depression
- Fever (usually 103-106°F)
- Swelling is present
- Tissues are red, swollen and warm
- Fluid within the swelling
- Painful to the touch
- Presence of a purulent discharge (pus)
- External wounds

NOTE - Symptoms usually develop 3-6 days after an injury has occurred. Contact your veterinarian when

- Wounds undetected earlier are now infected
- Skin and underlying tissues appear unhealthy and do not seem to be healing
- A purulent discharge (pus) develops or is detected coming from an area
- A sudden swelling appears, accompanied by a fever, depression and usually tenderness
- Drainage from an abscess stops and swelling begins in the area

Treatment

Infected wounds

- Clean the wound thoroughly with mild soap and water or a suitable antiseptic solution, such as povidone-iodine (Betadine).
- Apply an antibiotic ointment or powder. Apply the ointment or powder twice daily for 2 days and then once daily for 3 to 5 days

- Animals with puncture or extensive wounds should be given systemic antibiotics (available from a veterinarian)

Abscesses

- When abscesses are unopened but a scab is present, open the abscess by pulling off the scab. Clip the hair away from an unopened abscess and apply hot packs to the area to help make it "head"
- Apply pressure on both sides of the opening and expel the pus
- Clean both inside and outside thoroughly with an antiseptic, such as povidone iodine (Betadine) solution
- Keep the wound open by cleaning and applying an antibiotic ointment inside twice daily. The wound opening must be kept open for several days to allow healing from the inside out or the abscess is likely to form again
- Unopened abscesses should be surgically treated by a veterinarian

Prevention

- Encourage wound bleeding at the time of the injury by applying pressure around the wound
- Clean and treat fresh wounds promptly
- Treat puncture and extensive wounds immediately with antibiotics
- Seek veterinary services immediately after a serious injury

NOTES

#31 Scratching/Scooting

SCRATCHING

Scratching is not an extreme emergency but it can be disturbing to you and very uncomfortable for your pet. Self-mutilation caused by excessive biting and scratching can cause a minor lesion to become a very serious one within a few hours.

Causes

Parasites

- Fleas, mites, and lice
- Hookworms

Allergic Reactions

- Allergies
- Dermatitis
- Hives

Infections

- Secondary bacterial infections
- Moist eczema

Contact dermatitis (detergents, chemicals, paints)

Generalized skin diseases

Nutritional deficiencies (fats, vitamins)

Signs

- Biting and scratching of the skin
- Detection of fleas, lice
- Reddish-brown staining of the hair, caused by excessive licking
- Red or inflamed skin
- Small bumps or scabs
- Sticky, oozing areas
- Dandruff-like scabs
- Abnormally oily skin which has a rancid odor
- Hair loss
- Thickening of the skin

Contact your veterinarian when

- Scratching is frequent and persists. NOTE - It is normal for an animal to scratch 1 or 2 times a day, but not 2 to 3 times an hour.
- Skin damage becomes evident
- A sore area gets larger or appears to be infected

Treatment

Prevent self-mutilation by the animal

- Distract by exercising
- Apply an Elizabethan color or bucket (See Section #16 - Bandaging/Splints/Collars)
- Use tranquilizers (available from a veterinarian)
- Temporarily bandage the involved area
- Use medicated baths
- Clip hair and clean affected areas

- Cut the hair away from an infected or suppurating (moist eczema) lesion with clippers or blunt scissors
- A mild baby shampoo or soap can be diluted and used to bathe the area. Rinse and dry the area well
- Apply an antiseptic solution. Povidone-iodine (Betadine) scrub or solution can be used. Alcohol (70% ethyl or isopropyl) can be used successfully as an antibacterial agent on unbroken skin. Keep the skin wet for at least 2 minutes.

Treat the affected areas

- Use an antibiotic ointment or,
- Apply calamine lotion or a thick paste of baking soda and water

Obtain veterinary services when indicated.

Complications

- Self-mutilation
- Hair loss and skin damage
- Skin infections and lick sores may develop

Prevention

- Use proper flea control
- Grooming daily helps keep your pet's coat healthy and provides an opportunity to check its physical condition
- Periodic bathing of dogs helps maintain a healthy condition - cats rarely require bathing

SCOOTING

Causes

- Anal glands (sacs) that are impacted, infected or abscessed. The occurrence of impacted anal glands varies with the individual animal, but are more common in small breeds of dogs. Cats are infrequently affected. The anal sacs are located just under the skin on either side of the anus and open to the outside by means of a small duct. When the secretions become thick and cannot be expressed normally by the animal itself they are said to be impacted and if not relieved become infected and abscess.

IMPORTANT - Scooting is not a sign of worms except when they cause diarrhea and indirectly irritate the anal area.

Signs

- Dragging (scooting) of the anal area on the ground or floor
- Excessive licking of the anus IMPORTANT - You should suspect an anal gland problem when a pet drags its bottom on the floor for 2 or more days without getting relief

Treatment

- Manually massage the anal sacs, expressing their contents directly into a piece of cotton or disposable cloth. Pressure should be applied directly over the glands on each side of the anus
- Seek veterinary assistance to have glands completely expressed and checked for infection

#32 Urethral Obstruction

Synonyms

- Feline urological syndrome (feline only)
- Urethral blockage

Cause

- The obstruction is caused by sandy debris, mucus, crystals or stones that lodge in the end of a male's urethra

Signs (early)

- Urinating in unusual places, such as a sink or bathtub
- Urinating small amounts
- Excessive squatting and straining
- Blood in the urine
- Licking and protrusion of the penis

Signs (late)

- Meowing or crying frequently
- Abdomen is usually painful when touched
- Vomiting and/or depression

IMPORTANT - A cat with urinary tract obstruction may die if the condition is not corrected within 48 hours. The signs of urethral obstruction in a cat or dog are similar to the signs of constipation. If laxatives are used when the animal has an urethral obstruction, it may contribute to rupturing a distended bladder.

Treatment

- Veterinary assistance must be obtained immediately
- An anesthetic and catheterization are often required

Prevention

- The various methods of prevention are beyond the scope of this book, but should be discussed in detail with your pet's doctor

32.

#33 Vomiting/Motion Sickness

VOMITING

Definition

Vomiting is the forcible expulsion of stomach contents through the mouth. It is not a disease entity in itself, but rather a symptom of a digestive disorder or an underlying disease.

Signs

- Restlessness
- Salivation
- Frequent swallowing
- Licking lips
- Abdominal muscular contractions
- Expulsion of material from the mouth

Causes

Dietary

- Overeating or eating too fast
- Exercise on a full stomach
- Change in diet
- Ingestion of grass or spoiled food
- Swallowing undigestible objects

Emotional

- Excitement or fear
- Pain
- Motion sickness
- Brain injuries

Specific Diseases

- Stomach disease
- Throat irritations
- Generalized or metabolic disease
- Intestinal obstructions

Other

- Acute abdominal injuries
- Parasites
- Poisons
- Drugs

IMPORTANT - The first material vomited may contain a clue to the cause and should be examined carefully.

Do not be concerned if your dog or cat occasionally vomits. Re-ingestion of occasional vomitus is considered a normal part of digestion in many carnivore animals.

NOTE - Gagging may easily be confused with vomiting, but in general it is less serious. Gagging produces a phlegm-like fluid rather than food or bile colored (yellow to greenish-yellow) fluid as in vomiting

Consult a veterinarian after

- 6 hours when vomiting is very frequent or other signs accompany it such as depression, fever or diarrhea
- 12 hours when vomiting persists or reoccurs

Do not attempt to treat or wait when

- Blood is present
- Vomiting is projective (extremely forceful)
- Abdominal pain is present, as detected by applying gentle pressure to the abdomen
- Abdominal distension is present

Treatment

- Withhold all water for 12 hours (adult animals only)
- Withhold all food for 24 hours (adult animals only)
- Treat medically by using one of the following:
  - Intestinal protectives (Kaopectate or Pepto-Bismol), administer orally 2 teaspoons (l0 cc) per 10 lbs. of body weight every 2-6 hours
  - Antacid liquids (Maalox or Mylanta), administer orally 1 teaspoon (5 cc) per 20 lbs. of body weight every 8 hours
- Reintroduce water slowly in small amounts; 1 tablespoon per 10 lbs. of body weight every hour or place several ice cubes in a bowl for the animal to lick.

NOTE - Puppies and kittens should be given a mixture of 1/2 teaspoon (2.5cc) of table salt and 1 tablespoon (15cc) of sugar mixed in 1 quart of water.

- Begin feeding a soft bland diet, (See Section #15 - Diarrhea) broth or baby foods in small amounts several times a day. Gradually return to normal feedings during the next 1 to 2 days
- Consult a veterinarian when the condition exists for more than a few hours

Prevention

- Avoid exercising your pet immediately after eating
- Prevent overeating by restricting the amount of food given during each feeding
- Encourage slower eating by feeding large

chunks of food that have to be chewed and by feeding separate from other animals

MOTION SICKNESS

Some animals, particularly puppies, may become nauseated and vomit when they ride in automobiles, boats and airplanes. Most cats manifest motion sickness and fear by excessive drooling without vomiting. Animals usually outgrow the problem of motion sickness.

Signs

- Restlessness
- Excessive salivation (drooling)
- Panting with frequent swallowing
- Vomiting

Treatment

- Use an antiemetic drug (prevents nausea and vomiting) obtained from a veterinarian
- Use one of the following antiemetic drugs which are available from your pharmacist or veterinarian as a non-prescription drug. Give the drug one hour before traveling

DRUGS USED FOR MOTION SICKNESS IN DOGS AND CATS

Drug	Oral Dosage*	Frequency
Dimenhydrinate (Dramamine)	0.5 mg.	Every 8 hours if needed
Meclizine hydrochloride (Bonine)	1 to 2 mg.	Every 24 hours if needed

*Per Pound of Body Weight

References: 11, 17, 20

#34 Orphans

Milk should be present at the time of birth and production should increase during the first 24 hours after delivery. A newborn animal should receive some of this first milk (colostrum). This provides temporary immunity against some diseases and it contains extra nutrition.

Causes

- Mother becomes lost, ill or dies
- Litter is larger than the mother can care for
- Mother may reject one or more of her offspring
- Inadequate amount of milk
- Infected milk
- Babies are too weak to nurse
- Babies are too small to compete with larger littermates
- Babies are delivered by cesarean section

Normal Babies Should

- Be quiet between feedings
- Sleep most of the time when not nursing
- Suck vigorously after tasting milk
- Have stools that are formed
- Have from 3 to 6 bowel movements daily

Provide a Proper Environment

- Maintain the temperature and humidity at a constant level, while avoiding any drafts. The heat should be thermostatically controlled and the humidity maintained between 40% and 50%. IMPORTANT - Chilling is one of the major causes of death in newborn animals. Keep puppies and kittens warm. Few can recover from a severe initial chill.

- Maintain these temperatures

AGE	TEMPERATURE
l week	85-90°F
2 weeks	80-85°F
3 weeks	75-80°F
4 weeks	70-75°F

NOTE - Whenever another milk producing mother is available and will accept an orphan, take advantage of this opportunity.

Feeding a Proper Formula

- Commercial Milk Formula for Puppies
  Esbilac (Borden) - This product is available from veterinarians or pet stores and is an excellent replacement for mother's milk.

ESBILAC FORMULA

Age	Calories Needed Daily Per lb. Body Weight	Quantity Required Daily Per lb. Body Weight
1 week	60	2 oz. (60cc)
2 weeks	70	2 l/3 oz. (70cc)
3 weeks	80	3 2/3 oz. (80cc)
4 weeks	100	3 1/3 oz. (100cc)

Feed these amounts of formula divided into 3 or 4 feedings a day at 6 to 8 hour intervals. Small or weak puppies should be fed every 2 to 3 hours.

- Evaporated Milk Emergency Formula for Puppies consists of 5 parts evaporated milk, 1 part boiled water, 1 teaspoon dicalcium phosphate per quart of liquid. This formula supplies 35 calories per ounce and should be fed at the same rate as Esbilac (See above)
- Whole Milk Emergency Formula for Puppies consists of 2 egg yolks and 8 ounces homogenized milk. Feed 2 times the amount of the formulas listed above in order to provide an equal amount of calories, protein, calcium and phosphorus
- A good commercial milk formula for kittens if KMR (Kitten Milk Replacer). This product is available from veterinarians or pet stores and is an excellent replacement for mother's milk

KMR (Kitten Milk Replacer)

Weight in Ounces	**Amount Fed Per Day** (Tablespoons)
3	1.5
4	2.5
6	3
8	4
10	6
12	7
14	8

Feed these amounts of formula, divided into 3 or 4 feedings a day at 6 to 8 hour intervals. Small or weak kittens should be fed every 2 to 3 hours.

- Whole Milk Emergency Formula for Kittens consists of 4 ounces of homogenized milk, I hard boiled egg, I teaspoon of powdered calcium carbonate and liquid vitamins (follow

package directions). Mix in a blender until smooth. Refrigerate between feedings. Feed twice as much of this as the KMR.
NOTE - Use only as a temporary measure until a commercial diet can be obtained.

Formula Feeding Suggestions

- Mix the formula well and warm to 100°F (body temperature) before feeding
- Avoid nursing too rapidly. The milk should drip slowly from the nipple when the bottle is inverted. Enlarge the hole in the nipple with a hot needle if necessary
- Place the baby on its stomach and slip the nipple over the top of its tongue. Keep a slight pull on the bottle to encourage sucking
- Burp the baby after each feeding by holding it against your shoulder and rubbing and patting its back
- Wipe the anal and abdominal areas with a warm moist cloth after each feeding to stimulate elimination. Start pan feeding at 3 weeks of age by mixing the milk replacer with small amounts of solid food. Make this or any diet change gradually. Spoon-feeding for a short period may help start the diet conversion

IMPORTANT - Slight underfeeding is preferable to overfeeding, especially the first 2 or 3 days. If diarrhea occurs, reduce the next feeding by one half the amount previously fed and then gradually increase to an amount that does not cause diarrhea

Contact a Veterinarian When

- The baby whines or cries excessively
- The baby refuses food at normal feedings
- The baby has loose stools that persist for more than 3 or 4 feedings
- There is no increase in the baby's body weight every few days
- You have any questions regarding an orphan or its feeding

References: 14, 16

NOTES

#35 Restraint/Transportation

MOUTH TIE RESTRAINT

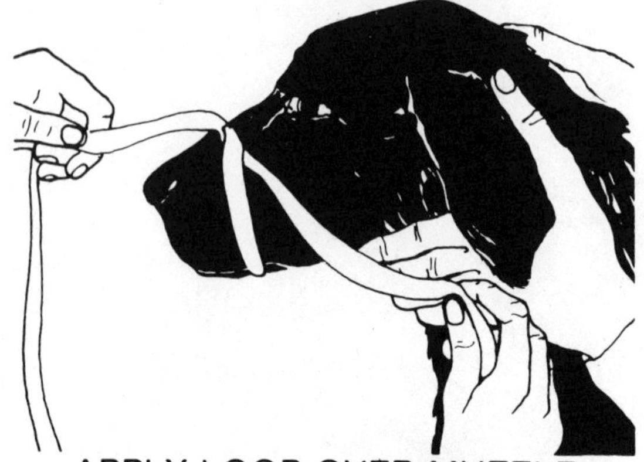

APPLY LOOP OVER MUZZLE

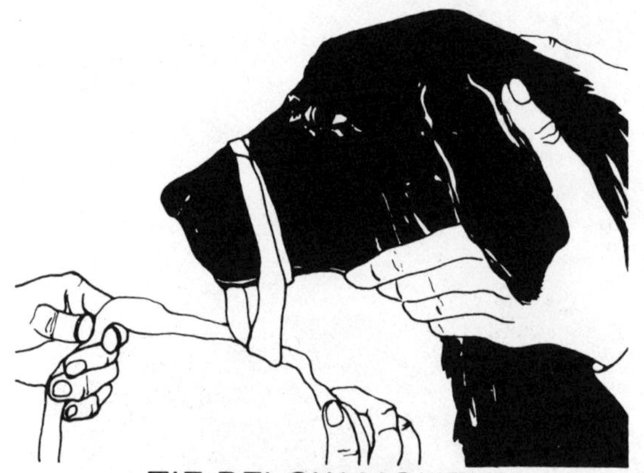

TIE BELOW MOUTH

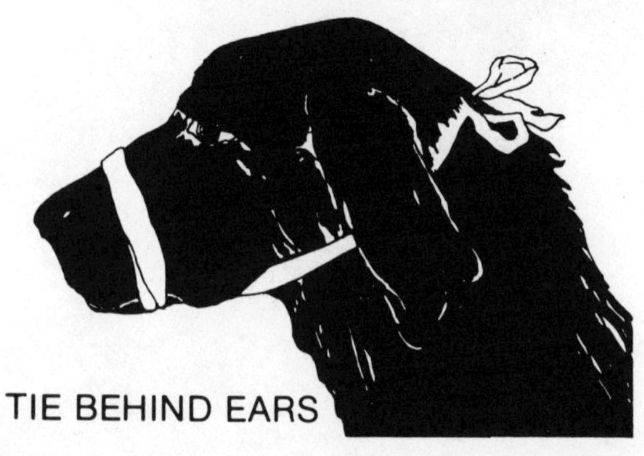

TIE BEHIND EARS

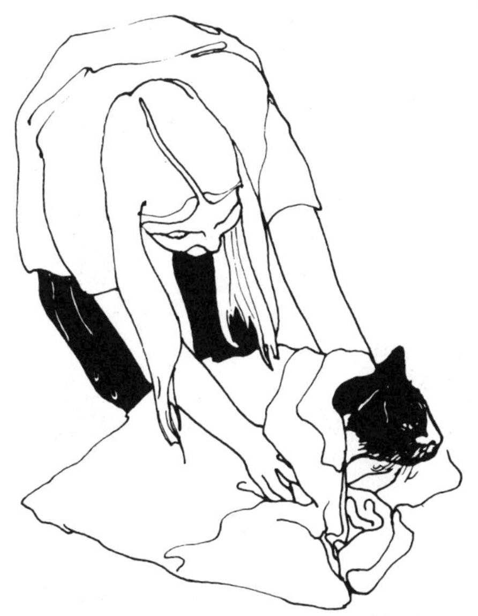

RESTRAINING AN INJURED CAT OR SHORT MUZZLED DOG WITH A COAT OR BLANKET

CARRYING A CAT OR SHORT MUZZLED DOG RESTRAINED IN A TOWEL

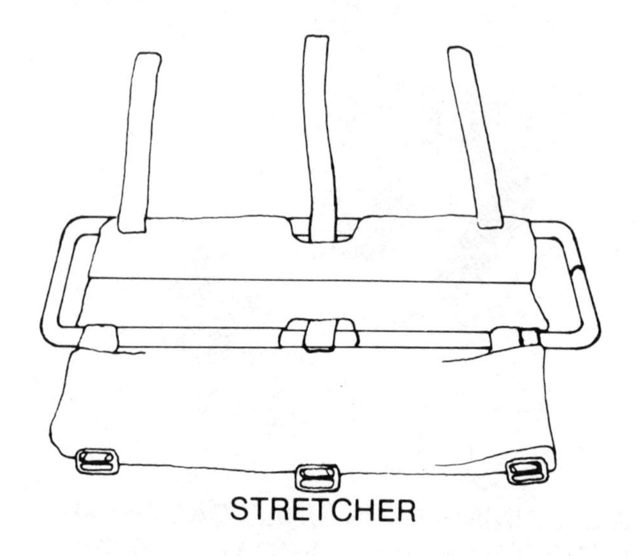

STRETCHER

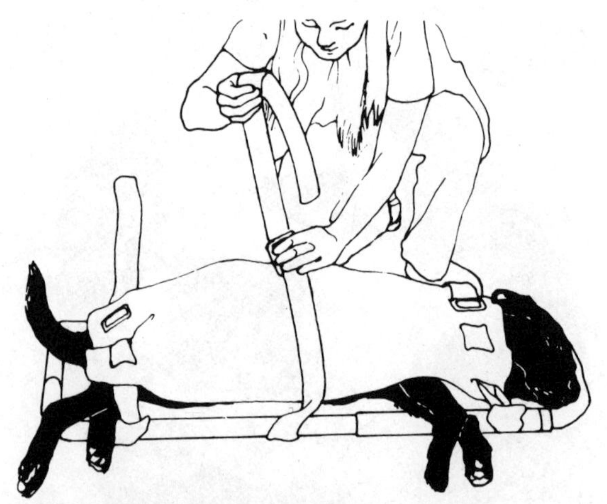

STRAPPING IN AN INJURED DOG

CARRYING A CAT

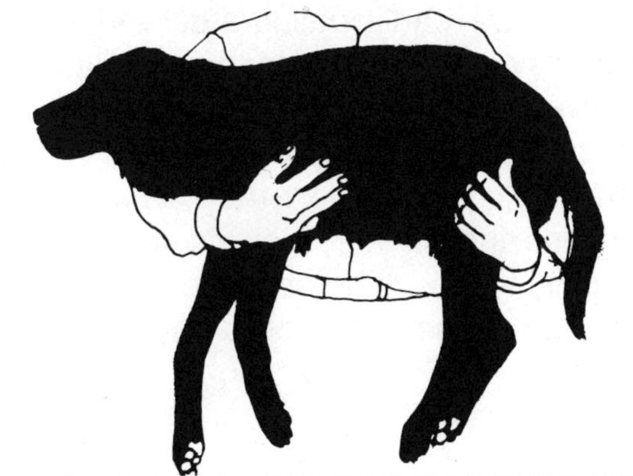

METHODS OF CARRYING INJURED DOGS

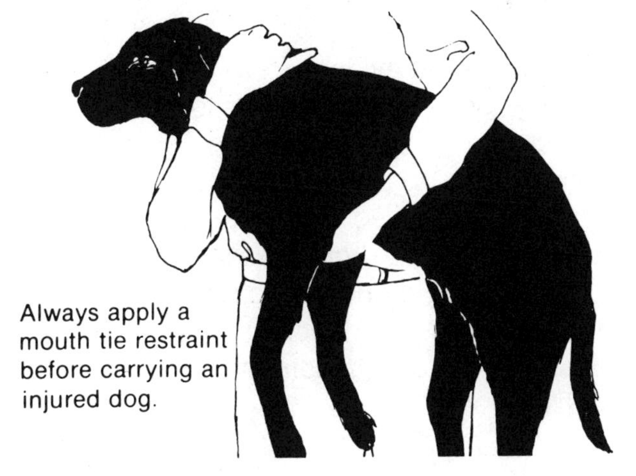

Always apply a mouth tie restraint before carrying an injured dog.

#36 Whelping/Queening

Whelping denotes normal birth or parturition in a member of the canine family.

Queening or kindling are terms used to denote normal birth or parturition in a member of the feline family.

Interfering with normal parturition is usually unnecessary and undesirable. However, being aware of how a delivery is progressing and giving assistance, if needed, may save not only the babies but also the mother. Confusion and strangers should not be allowed during the delivery. You should start anticipating a delivery on about the 58th day of pregnancy for dogs or cats. Begin recording the mother's temperature twice daily at this point (normal temperature 101.5 F 1). When the temperature falls below 100°F it is a good time to exercise the animal. Make sure she has an opportunity to relieve herself before labor begins, but be careful she does not run off at this time.

Signs

First Stage

- Restlessness is evident
- "Nesting" occurs. The pet tries to make a bed or nest
- Seeks seclusion and may in fact hide
- May vomit or refuse food
- Body temperature drops below 100°F several hours before the onset of labor
- Milk may drop from nipples
- External genitalia becomes prominent and flaccid

- A white vaginal discharge which comes from the cervical seal may be present
- Panting and trembling

Second Stage

- Perceptible and forceful abdominal contractions occur approximately one hour before delivery
- Straw colored fluid may be seen
- Greenish watery sac may protrude from the vulva opening
- Straining and expulsion of babies occurs
- The placenta (afterbirth) is passed now or shortly after birth

NOTE - The animal may rest for a few minutes to one or more hours before proceeding with labor. A normal delivery may take up to 24 hours from the time the first puppy or kitten until the last.

Contact Your Veterinarian

During Labor When

- Pregnancy lasts more than 65 days
- Any stage of labor is longer than 3 hours
- No delivery occurs within 4 hours after onset of labor
- Strong persistent labor occurs for 30 minutes without a birth
- Weak intermittent labor occurs for 6 hours without a birth
- Contractions do not reoccur after 1 or 2 babies and there is a 4 hour lapse since the last birth
- A visible baby cannot be gently removed

- Greenish-black discharge is present but no birth or labor contractions occur within the next 3 hours
- Severe bright red bleeding occurs
- Excessive urination occurs with contractions

After Labor When

- Babies cry excessively. A healthy baby will either be nursing or sleeping
- Milk is absent or discolored
- Breasts are hard, discolored or painful
- When a vaginal discharge persists beyond 2 weeks or is large in amount or odorous or is any color other than a normal dark red

NOTE - It is recommended that a veterinarian check the babies within the first 24-48 hours.

Care of a Newborn Animal

- Remove any membranes covering the baby. The membranes usually break during birth or the mother removes them
- Clean the face, removing mucus or fluids from the mouth or nose
- Rub with a clean dry towel to stimulate breathing and circulation
- Gently swing the baby with its head down while supporting the head in your hand (See illustration Page168).This helps remove fluids still in the lungs and air passages and stimulates breathing. The baby should begin to squirm and cry
- If breathing does not occur, place your mouth over the puppies nose and blow gently to ex-

pand the chest. Gentle chest massage may also be indicated
- Hold the placenta above the baby for 2 or 3 minutes to let any blood run out
- Tie the umbilical cord with a fine piece of thread or unwaxed dental floss. The distance the tie is made from the body should be 1/2 inch in kittens and l inch in puppies. Cut the cord between the placenta and the tie with a pair of scissors (disinfect scissors between puppies)
- Dip the cord in a cup or dish of disinfectant solution. Use Betadine, 3% Iodine or rubbing alcohol

NOTE - A placenta should be passed with each baby delivered.

Assisting With A Delivery

A normal delivery should be complete within l5 minutes after part of the puppy or kitten becomes visible.

- Clean the vulva with a mild disinfectant
- Wash your hands and lubricate a finger with white petroleum jelly, Vaseline or K-Y jelly
- Lubricate the birth canal by inserting the finger and gently moving it around the baby
- Grasp the legs and/or the skin on the back with a towel or piece of cloth. Avoid pulling on the head
- Apply gentle, steady traction simultaneously with the mother's contractions. Do not jerk or pull suddenly
- Pull downward toward the mother's feet and not straight back

- When the head is too large to fit through the vulva manipulate the edges of the vulva around the head
- If a placenta remains in the birth canal, grasp it with a cloth and pull gently but firmly

IMPORTANT - Failure to deliver the baby in 4-5 minutes indicates the need for immediate veterinary assistance.

NOTE - Ingestion of I or 2 placental membranes by the mother causes little or no harm. Consumption of a large number of membranes may cause vomiting and diarrhea.

Complications

- Hemorrhage
- Babies or membranes are retained
- Infection of the uterus (metritis or pyometra)
- Infection of the mammary glands (mastitis or abscess development)
- Shock (See Section #26 - Shock)

References: 2, 17, 19, 20

SWINGING A NEWBORN ANIMAL TO REMOVE FLUIDS FROM THE LUNGS

NOTES

When Pets Die

Signs

- Cessation of breathing
- Absence of a heartbeat (See Section #4 Cardiac Arrest/Cardiopulmonary Resusitation)
- Dilated pupils which are non-responsive to light
- Loss of eyeball firmness
- Spontaneous passing of urine and feces may occur
- Muscles become limp
- Cooling of the body occurs in 1-2 hours
- Rigor mortis or stiffening of muscles usually occurs after several hours

The disposition of the body of a dear pet and companion is always an unpleasant task. All too frequently, it is done in an improper and unesthetic manner. Determining what is the proper method in your area can usually be done by contacting one of the following:

- Animal Shelter or Dog Pound
- Humane Society
- City Police Department/Sheriff's Office
- Veterinarian
- Wildlife Conservation Officer

Methods of Disposition

- Burial - Sometimes an individual can and prefers to bury his own pet. This requires an acceptable location. In many metropolitan and heavily populated areas this is not only difficult, but it is unlawful due to potential public health hazards. Proper disposition of animals under these circumstances should be available through some local agency.

- Cremation - Facilities are available in many areas to have your pet's remains cremated. The ashes usually can be saved for your personal disposition, if you so choose. Your local animal warden or veterinarian will know if facilities for cremation are available.

- Pet cemeteries - These facilities are available in many metropolitan areas

REFERENCES

1. American Academy of Orthopedic Surgeons, Emergency Care and Transportation of the Sick and Injured, Chicago, Illinois, Amer. Aca. Ortho. Surg., 1977.
2. American Kennel Club Board of Directors, The Complete Dog Book, 16th Ed., New York, Howell Book House, 1982.
3. American National Red Cross, Standard First Aid and Personal Safety. Doubleday and Company, Inc., Garden City, NY, 1975.
4. Atkins, C. E., Johnson, R. K.: Clinical Toxicities of Cats. In Oehme, F. W. (ed.): Veterinary Clinics of North America, Vol. 5, No. 4, Nov. 1975. Philadelphia, W. B. Saunders Co.
5. Bailey, E. M.: Emergency Procedures in Intoxications. In Oehme, F. W. (ed.): Veterinary Clinics of North America, Vol. 5, No. 4, Nov. 1975. Philadelphia, W. B. Saunders Co.
6. Behler, J. L. , King, F. W.: The Audubon Society Field Guide to North American Reptiles and Amphibians. New York, Alfred A. Knopf, 1979.
7. Calsow, D.: Cats Question Box, P. 14-15, Cats Magazine, Dec., 1977.
8. Case, A. A.: Beautiful but Deadly. Lincoln, Ne., Norden Laboratories, Winter, 1973.
9. Dowlen, R.: Removing Stains From Fabrics. Washington, D.C., U.S. Government Printing Office, 1977.
10. Fowler, M. E.: Plant Poisoning in Small Companion Animals. St. Louis, MO, Ralston Purina Co., 1981.
11. Gellis, S. S., Kagan, B. M.: Current Pediatric Therapy 7, Philadelphia, W. B. Saunders Co., 1976.

12. Green, M. I.: A Sigh of Relief - The First-Aid Handbook of Childhood Emergencies. Bantam Books, Inc., 1977.
13. Hoerlein, B. F.: Canine Neurology, 3rd Ed. Philadelphia, W. B. Saunders Co., 1978.
14. Kirk, R. W. (ed.): Current Veterinary Therapy VIII. Philadelphia, W. B. Saunders Co., 1983.
15. Kirk, R. W. (ed.): Current Veterinary Therapy IX. Philadelphia, W. B. Saunders Co., 1986.
16. Kirk, R. W.: First Aid for Pets, New York, E. P. Dutton, 1978.
17. Kirk, R. W., Bistner, S. I.: Handbook of Veterinary Procedures and Emergency Treatment, 4th Ed., Philadelphia, W. B. Saunders Co., 1985.
18. Kovsky, M. L.: Cat and Dog First Aid Guide Developed for Emergencies. Portland, Animal Care Publications, Inc., 1975.
19. McGinnis, Terri: The Well Dog Book, New York, Random House, Inc. and Berkeley, The Bookworks, 1977.
20. McGinnis, Terri: The Well Cat Book, New York, Random House, Inc. and Berkeley, The Bookworks, 1975.
21. Oehme, F. W., Toxicologic Problems, In Ettinger, S. J. (ed.): Textbook of Veterinary Internal Medicine, 2nd Ed., Philadelphia, W. B. Saunders Co., 1983.
22. Paddleford, R. R., Short, C. E., McGrath, C. J., Cardiopulmonary Resuscitation. In the Practicing Veterinarian: Vol. 47, No. 4, Oct/Nov 1975. Washington Crossing, N.J., Pitman-Moore, Inc.
23. Pinniger, R.S.(ed.): Jones's Animal Nursing. 2nd Ed. Oxford, England, Pergamon Press, 1976.

24. Poisindex: Englewood, Co., Micromedics, Inc., 1984.
25. Renshaw, C. C. (ed.): The American Medical Associations's Handbook of First Aid and Emergency Care. New York, Random House, 1980.
26. Ryan, C. P.: First Aid, Part 2, p. 24-25, Today's Animal Health, May/June 1977.
27. Strowe, C. M.: Small Animal Intoxications. White Plains, N.Y., Gaines Progress, Summer and Fall 1981.
28. Yeary, R. A.: Syrup of Ipecac as an Emetic in the Cat. J.A.V.M.S., 161:1677, 1972.